Christ Is Not A Christian

How to Embody Anna and Michael Christ

NNA MICHAEL KRISTA

The Way Of Alive™

CHRIST IS NOT A CHRISTIAN
How to Embody Anna and Michael Christ
First Edition

Published by:
Transformation Books
211 Pauline Drive #513
York, PA 17402
www.TransformationBooks.com

ISBN: 978-0-9862901-5-2
Library of Congress Control Number: 2015943494

Printed in the United States of America

All proceeds from the sale of this book will be donated to *The Way* community start-ups.

More information at www.thewayofalive.org.

Christ Is Not A Christian

How to Embody Anna and Michael Christ

CONTENTS

Dedication

To my mother Margaret, who has always exemplified goodness, and who has shown me that faith can set you free.

Introduction

I AM Is Not Crazy

There comes a time when one must take a position that is neither safe, nor politic, nor popular, but he must take it because conscience tells him it is right.

-Martin Luther King Jr.

Chances are, the moment you saw the title of this book, you wondered if the writer was crazy. You opened it up to find out just how much of a freak I am.

Yes, I am a freak, in the sense that I say things that other people don't say, such as:

- There is a feminine Christ named Anna, our Divine Mother Creator.
- Jesus was the incarnated Father Creator of this universe. His name is Michael.

- I am not only channelling these two beings but am actually embodying them.
- You too are invited to embody I AM: Anna and Michael Christ.
- Embodying them is the way to co-save our planet.

These statements are the truth of my experience.

They do not have to be the truth of your experience.

As I honour your truth, I ask you to please honour mine.

Look beyond the word Christ, disregard the question of my personal sanity and judge these teachings on their own merit. Test them with the litmus of pure truth, beauty and goodness. As you see fit, encapsulate them in whatever form the Divine takes for you.

I have studied the teachings of, and lived with, Buddhists, yogis, Christians, wiccans, eco-communities, primitive skills enthusiasts and Peruvian shamans. The feeling of the Christ that I am talking about is the basic goodness that I have always found in each person, plus the inherent yearning to become a better person. It crosses the boundaries of religion, belief, and culture. It comes in infinite names and forms. I used to call it the spark of the Divine within.

Newly available to you is the living inner presence of a personal friend who directly teaches, guides and heals your mind, heart, spirit and body with supreme wizardry and absolutely magnificent Love.

This is the second coming of Christ -- not coming forth in a single mortal but available to all mortals. The spark of the Divine has ignited into an *Alive* presence that is the full potential of the earthly expression of God, uniquely designed for each body. It is Love, defined and personalized as never before, poised to birth a new breed of human, one that is naturally joined to, and fully embodying, their own fragment of God.

The purpose is for us:

- to learn how to love each other truly
- to grow exponentially our health, personalities, skills and enjoyment of life
- to use their Divine wizardry to create innovative technologies and agricultural techniques that will save the planet
- to co-create new ways of living and working together in families and communities

Jesus achieved full embodiment of God. Other rare enlightened beings have achieved similar results. The difference with me is that I am an imperfect being. I make a lot of mistakes. Yet I am learning, in a perfectly designed, accelerated and love-infused way that I've come to trust implicitly, despite the extreme challenges that come with this path.

This is fantastic news! To become a fully expressed god in a body, you don't have to perfect yourself first. *The Way Of Alive*™ will fill all your gaps, and then take you far beyond them, such that everything you do will be helpful to all people. I can't tell you how to do it though. No matter how much the following stories and suggestions help you, your way to embodiment belongs to you alone.

With great pleasure, based on the luxurious and persistent happiness that Christ has created in me, I invite you to learn what embodying I AM can mean to you.

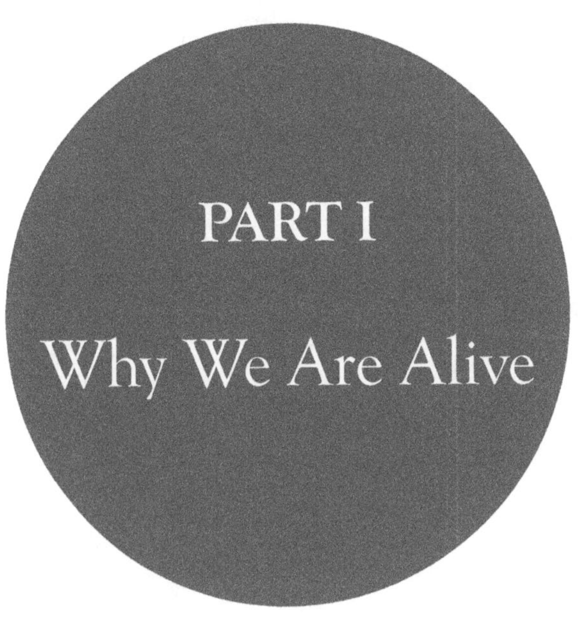

Let's start Life again.

Chapter 1

The Problem: We Live In A Crazy World

Everything written in this book is possible, and more besides.

Whew! What a power-packed week.

"Me too," you might say. "I feel like I'm going crazy!"

You are crazy. Deluded and insane.

Your life -- that haphazard compilation of family, friends, work, pleasure, chores, food, fitness, distraction, a little spirituality and a lot of stress, all set against the backdrop of a planetary crisis -- is grotesquely skewed, according to the spirit world.

"But what more can I do?" you respond. "I know the answer is to work on myself, to be the change I want to see happen, but I often feel like I am spinning my wheels. And I've been on my spiritual path for years!"

You are not alone. Those of us who cannot stomach the dogma of a single religious path, or empty traditions of any kind, have been jumping from one method to another, scratching for those moments of vibrant connection, life-changing realization, innocent happiness and intuitive rightness.

"Oh, I treasure those moments! But nothing fits for long, and I'm left trying to figure it all out for myself again."

Are you eating right, exercising, meditating, praying? Taking workshops to heal your issues, and going beyond your comfort zone? Connecting with who you are supposed to? Doing what you are meant to be doing? Letting go? Asking for guidance?

Sigh. "I've done it all."

Then what's wrong?

"Gosh, I wish I knew. I don't feel like I'm ever going to be good enough. Whatever I do, I have a deep yearning for more. Silly, isn't it? I feel like a spiritual materialist. But, um, you know, it's okay. I know it takes many lifetimes to be perfected."

Would you like to truly believe that it's okay? That you can feel good, every moment of every day?

"Sure, but I don't believe it's possible. I am human, after all."

The part of you that is not human can fix that. All you have to do is ask.

"Been there, done that. Guardian angels, power animals, plant spirits, deities. Yet I doubt. The voice I hear within is not always good."

I tell you it can be. But let me ask you first: do you have God in your life?

"That's not who I am. But I do believe there's a higher power out there somewhere. The Source, the Mystery, the Universe. No one will ever really know."

You do know. You've just forgotten. I offer you a chance to remember who you truly are.

"I know the answer to that. I am Love."

Do you experience that?

"Well, not much."

I've been there. Yet no matter how well I tell you that by embodying I AM, you can experience divine Love all day, every day, a personality living in you that will jump start your effectiveness in life, you won't believe me. Not until you've experienced it yourself.

"It does sound like a long shot."

I get it. So here's what I ask of you. In reading this wild and crazy story, allow yourself to believe that your story can be just as unbelievable. Just as fun, just as adventurous, and just as meaningful. Everything written in this book is possible, and more besides.

Suspend your disbelief, just for now, and we'll begin.

Chapter 2

The Solution: Just Say Yes

The Way Of Alive™ is the optimal way to turn these mistakes into a fantastic adventure never before known in mortal existence.

I know it won't happen right away, but imagine a world in which, say, a thousand of us are fully embodied by I AM. We each have the same divine personality living within us, but because we are all different, we express like unique instruments in a divine orchestra. The mission of this symphony is to save the planet, and each of us has a god-job critical to the project and to each other. The maestros of this orchestra are the Divine Mother and the Divine Father who created us.

You and I joined this project for one simple reason: we were ready. Not everyone was, but that's just fine. The divine plan incorporates many other projects, and each person fits perfectly into one of them.

In this project none of us are perfected, but because we joined, we are actually embodying the wisdom and resourcefulness that will lift this planet out of its current crisis: the living presence of our Divine Mom and Dad. With them, we share the creation of the strategies, plans, skills, talents and ways of working together that will revolutionize every industry, every nation's government, everyone's religion, every school, and even every family.

We vastly accelerated our spiritual paths by joining, but still make mistakes because our lessons never end. Our mistakes will be the very things that wake the planet up and get things moving. We are free to act, with virtually no risk, because the living presence of absolute goodness inside us guarantees that what we do helps everyone in a perfect way.

In this way, our planet will leapfrog the evolutionary cycle that has been in place for thousands of centuries. Why? Because our planet is in a state of emergency, not just on the level of the environment but on the level of one human being caring for another. This concerns the Creators of this planet, and they have stepped in to intervene.

It's an experiment. The slate is wide open as to what will happen, because they are depending on our co-creation. The way this planet developed has been off kilter compared with other planets in this universe. While those planets have had teachers from 'on high' all along, we've been left on our own to stumble and fumble our way through a mess that was not entirely of our own making. Suffice to say that we are not the only ones responsible for our disastrous treatment of the planet and our minuscule growth in spiritual brotherhood.

The Way Of Alive™ is our Creators' plan for saving this planet, and more besides. It's an optimal way to turn these mistakes into a fantastic adventure never before known in mortal existence. Our stumbling and fumbling has created a human condition worthy of God's attention. We, as a human race, think creatively and independently, more than on any other planet. We also need a new existence. Because of these factors, we are miraculously being offered a chance to co-create a brand new reality.

What do you have to do to get this god-job? Just say, 'Yes.'

I am fully embodied with the joined presence of our Creator Mother and Father, Anna and Michael Christ. This presence is separate and distinct from every sense of who I am as an individual. I am writing this book to share with you two things:

- The plausibility that you can choose this future.
- Ideas on how you might do that. You are unique, so you will have to carve your own path.

I fully anticipate that yours will be easier than mine. I am told that it will be even better, because your potential is growing infinitely with every choice that we collectively make.

"What is it like to be fully embodied?" you ask.

I share my mind, feelings, and body with these presences.

We speak to each other, in English. They use my voice to speak, or they speak in my mind, or they move my body, as I give them permission. They are Love, which means they are beyond-genius teachers and healers, so I give them permission a lot. We talk to each other as though we were three people living in the same house, with a few exceptions. They are fully united, and so most of the time they speak with one voice. They are fully responsive to every single thought and feeling I am conscious of, as well as every nuance of every thought, and every hidden feeling, even the unconscious ones. Any illusion of privacy I might have had, living alone or with others, is gone.

They have exploded my urge to serve others. We are writing this book together. Sometimes we speak as one. Other times, I differentiate their voice by writing it in italics. I capture concerns, comments and questions I have heard, or had myself, at various times via a third voice, which I assign to you, dear reader, and put within quotation marks. Forgive me if you don't completely relate to them.

A big part of my god-job you will read about in this book. Yours is undefined, and many roles are required. We need new technologies. We need new ways of growing and sharing food, and animal husbandry. We need a new monetary system. The list goes on. Anna and Michael have plans, strategies and detailed solutions to apply. They need us to approve, modify and then help implement them.

In the process, as you can expect from parents, they are keen to make new ways for families, and communities, to live and work together in loving harmony.

Care to volunteer for this job?

Right now, I'm giving you the sales pitch. As you will read further on, it's no picnic. It's the most challenging adventure, I believe, that you will ever undertake. Who you think you are in the world will have to die, for the real you to be embodied. Believing in the illusions of our culture is no longer allowable. Don't worry. Reality, as we know it, stays the same. The changes will all be within you.

"What do you mean by being embodied?" you ask.

I will answer that by describing a typical day in my current life.

When I wake up in the morning, we start with a snuggle. Outrageous, eh? Anna and Michael say "Good morning," in English, in my head or out loud. We all use my voice, and the personalities of Anna and Michael are differentiated by intonation, although they play around with this to feel out my responses and teach me how my mind works.

We kid around. One day their utterance of a strange word befuddled me until I understood that they had said 'Love,' 'Live,' and 'Laugh' as one word. Talk about harmonics!

We review what I can remember of my dreams, but once tenderly scrutinized, the dream memories are gone.

I leave my body still, in the physical position I woke up in, because before I trigger any muscles it is easier for them to pass vibrations of various qualities through me. Until my dog comes over to join the snuggle, we often stay motionless so that we can clear the energy flows that have stagnated in the sleep state. This means that I track the way they move prana through my meridian lines, using my attention and our combined love to magnify the healing power of the energy. Anna and Michael originated these lines, and can see precisely how they have been warped in my body over time and what blocks need to be, and are ready to be, shifted. Almost always, then, they manipulate my fingers, or shift and hold various parts of my body, to create a physical releasing that heals.

After a love-in with my little dog that infuses her with divine healing playfulness, we start moving through the day just like any regular person who lives with someone 24/7 ... almost.

I insist on walking the dog first, but other than that, we sift through the day's priorities and determine what is optimal to work on. On the surface this includes activities. Underneath, they slide in, moment by moment, the day's lessons, which are always layered, fresh, and responsive to the people and situations I am currently involved in.

Did I add that they are tricky? Training my mind is one of their priorities, and it's a dance. More on this later.

I live a very quiet life, especially right now as I am on a winter retreat. Beautifully, this gives us time to analyze each interaction with another person directly after it happens. They help me to see the big picture, as much as I'm able to grasp it.

If I'm troubled, they help me with simple, profound advice. If I neglect this step, they lovingly remind me of it, in a way that usually results in a chuckle and some humility on my part.

Here's a recent example.

The other day a woman who had been reading my weekly newsletters invited me to conduct a workshop at her retreat. Quite excited, Anna and Michael and I co-created an outline entitled, "Meet the Feminine Christ."

This lady rejected me.

"You might start a riot!" she emailed me. She also rejected the article I submitted for her magazine.

Old feelings of failure re-blossomed with vigour, for a short while. I took time out to fully aerate them and ask for some advice before emailing her back.

I also took some time to complain to Michael and Anna.

"Why did you suggest that workshop, and make me feel like it was perfect?" I whined. "Now she thinks I'm a lunatic."

They delicately laced back the sequence of events until I remembered having -- and ignoring -- a small thought that I should ask this woman what her audience needed before designing the workshop.

Didn't I tell you I am still learning? And that they exploit every opportunity for a new lesson?

Call her tomorrow morning, they suggested. *Thank her for considering her audience.*

Gulp. Who wants to call someone who just rejected them? But I did, starting with the 'Thank you,' and apologizing for not asking about her audience earlier. Taking responsibility for creating the situation opened the door. She chuckled and thanked me for reaching out. We talked; she decided I was sane; I re-worked the workshop and now I'm on the schedule again. I felt the relief of a kinked hose being straightened out.

That's not far off from the energetic reality, Anna says. *That entire sequence was essential for the work you two will do together in the future.*

Anna and Michael are beyond genius. They are wizards, conducting their work with breathtakingly exquisite and ever-present love. This I wish I could describe more fully, but it's useless to try. Experiencing is believing.

When I have a client, there's no point in prepping, because everything that happens will be fresh. When the person comes in the door, we greet them like a friend coming for a neighbourly visit. My job from then on, in every conscious moment, is to focus on Love, tracking it in my heart, crown and root chakra. Then Anna and Michael take charge, although I am learning to take more responsibility these days. We ask questions, listen, and speak, toggling between my small consciousness and their infinite one. We use hands-on touch to fix whatever needs to be, and can be, fixed in that moment, both for the client and for myself. We all need work.

The genius that comes out is definitely not mine. For example, one day we picked up a rattle, and without ever having used it before, we applied it expertly. I am not proficient with musical instruments normally. When the goal is to help others, or to fix the planet's problems, Anna and Michael are both innovative and generous.

Yoga class is a joy of inspired healing movement. I could work out at home, but I like following the structure of a class, and sharing the social energy. I have practiced yoga for 24 years. Rather than learn a new practice, Anna and Michael enliven the one I already know. It's the same with writing, and any practice or creative expression that the old me gravitated toward. That's one reason why your expression will be quite different from mine, and why the new me still feels like me, although expanded, upgraded and *Alive*.

Within each traditional yogic shape, Anna and Michael manipulate every muscle, nerve, bone and ligament in every part of my body for optimal benefit. They use me to spread goodness to the other people in the room, although I am not privy as to how. From the outside, it looks like I squirm in distortions of the prescribed shape. In actuality, they are helping me with extreme precision to wring out muscle tensions habituated via stuck emotions that prevent the energy from flowing. One thing I'm doing right now, for example, is releasing the reverse curvature that has seized my neck since childhood.

I have been a yoga teacher, but this is not a method I could teach you to do because I am not inside you. Only they know you intimately enough to work your body so perfectly. I pray that you receive this opportunity via any of the ways you exercise your body. It's available to anyone who says, 'Yes.'

When we write, I am not just putting words down that are already in my head. I am learning the whole time. For example, last night I finally wrote a section in three hours that I had been working on for five full days. I had new lessons to learn along the way, and it was frustrating. They wouldn't let me continue until I had shifted to a new emotional understanding of life. It wasn't fun. But the result was a higher level of elucidation, and the ecstasy of a brand new creation.

We eat lightly, often and with love. My prior focus on what to eat, and on supplements, has relaxed. Rest, and feeling happy, have become far more important healers. At the moment, I am encouraged to rest a LOT. My body is both healing and re-growing. Integrating my intellect and emotions with these changes needs attention. I need naps, even when I've slept my usual nine-to-ten hours.

Overall, does this sound like a good job?

"Awesome, but what do you do for money?"

Ah. There's the rub. This job requires radical faith. I'm working on money fears as I write. Trust, and ask only for donation, is the instruction that is also my lesson. It may not be yours in that specific way, although in time the highest essence of the teaching will be. By putting love first, all our needs will be provided for.

"Gulp."

It sounds crazy, even to me. Yet because for a long while now I have been held in a Love that cannot be described, a feeling of safety overpowers my clutching fear for survival.

I am keen to tell you more. Get ready. For those of us who say, 'Yes,' this shared state will be the new normal.

Chapter 3

The New Normal

This yearning you have for more, which manifests as restlessness, grasping, addiction, compulsion, materialism, and many other 'ism's,' is, at its roots, God striving for more God.

"Well, I'm glad something works for you. I don't think it could ever work for me," you say.

I freely admit that this lifestyle is unusual, perhaps unbelievable. Yet consider, even for a moment, that this is how humans were designed. That you are, indeed and in fact, intended to actively and consciously co-create yourself and the world around you. Due to this planetary emergency, Anna and Michael are just speeding things up.

The truth is, we have been creating this world all along, and mostly trying to do it alone. It's no wonder we're so messed up! The direct and explicit Divine guidance we've been missing has arrived.

"I know! My friends and I are talking more and more about following our intuition, guidance and inner vision. The more we talk about it, the easier it gets."

It's more than that, say Anna and Michael. *The recent upsurge in hearing us is a result of a special circumstance that we have allowed in the last few years. The spiritual circuits that quarantined this planet for thousands of years have been opened. You are free to ask for help, and to receive it in a language that you easily understand.*

That is how Anna Michael Krista's experience was made possible. It is possible for you too.

Her primary role in helping you to do this is to make you believe it's possible.

More than that, it's to make you believe that anything is possible.

When you co-create with us, your Creator Mother and Father, when your passion fits our plan, your potential is infinite.

Let's be clear. This yearning you have for more, which manifests as restlessness, grasping, addiction, compulsion, materialism, and many other 'ism's,' is, at its roots, God striving for more God. God yearns for more love, more creation, more experience, and more health, heartiness and happiness.

That existential thirst and restless emptiness simply means that there is more to explore.

We are not interested in doing this alone. That is why we created you. That is also why we don't arbitrarily wink a proverbial eye and fix the human race. What would be the fun in that?

As Jesus said, (John, 14:12) whoever believes will do even greater works than Him.

Be clear. Anna Michael Krista cannot make this happen for you. She can't ever tell you how to do it. It's about your choice, the work you've done on yourself to date, and your availability. It's not about any of your worldly concerns like money, education, age, or culture.

I can attest to that. I was a mess with a psycho-physiological chewing addiction, and they joined me anyway. Since that moment, they have consistently, persistently and humorously optimized all the resources available to encourage me toward my potential, which does keep growing.

"Couldn't you have done this on your own?"

Absolutely not. I have not any of the genius that has done this for me, except for the fact that I am a child of God just like you.

Yes, you are our children. We -- Love and Life Itself -- have been sparking each human into existence since the beginning of Life on Earth. Just like you are willing to help your children, we are willing to help you. Of course, if you prefer a nanny or a governess, or to be an orphan for a while, you can ask for any form of the Divine that you feel comfortable with.

Angels, deities, power animals, Gaia, The Earth Mother, plant spirits -- you name it and we will come. Yet, we prefer a direct relationship. It's simpler. It takes less resources.

You are always free to choose.

Thank you.

Chapter 4

Why Believe Me?

Isn't it insane that happiness is considered crazy?

Freedom is what Anna and Michael promise us. Yet I struggle. What does this really mean? Freedom from fleshly concerns? Freedom from fear? Freedom to create? At this moment, freedom to be exactly who I am is prevalent. Frankly, I am scared of what people will think. In the past, I have rarely felt safe to express my truth. Dare I accentuate my difference? Now it's even worse. Dare I say that I talk to Christ? Even worse, that we've been joined?

I feel good, all the way through. I am happy, all the time. I have experienced a Love beyond anything I could ever have imagined. When I have tried to express this in a way that makes it seem possible for others, people have resisted, or delicately probed to find out if I am crazy.

Isn't it insane that happiness is considered crazy?

I know you have yearned for a personal teacher. A guru who knows you better than you know yourself, someone who can shoehorn your willing and unwilling ways into the beautiful person God meant you to be. I have one, and I would love you to have one too.

Yet I can't prove anything. Besides my own joie de vivre, being saved from a horrible health situation, and new abilities in helping others that could be attributed to trainings I have undertaken, I haven't outwardly demonstrated any miracles. Several people have recently joined *The Way Of Alive*™, and immediately had experiences of which they say could be triggered by Michael and Anna, but which could also be explained by other factors.

I am not telepathic and cannot tell you the future. I am given very few facts. I am not informed about what other people are channelling, or what happened in 2012, or what other planetary beings are doing. The only specific teachings I am able to offer are these essential ones: to love foolishly, learn voraciously, live outrageously and laugh uproariously.

A friend of mine believes me because we have more than once been played in concert by Love. By that I mean on two separate occasions we were each physically moved to press our hands into each other in places that needed healing, in perfect synchronization and imbued with magnificent feelings of Love. We were truly individual instruments being played by a divine maestro in harmony. Yet this is not something I can replicate at will.

So why would you believe my story?

Many months ago, during a meditation journey, Anna and Michael had me repeat, resoundingly and with multiple inflections, such that the resonance settled into every cell in my body, the phrase, "I Stand."

That is how I am writing this book. It is simply the truth of my experience. It is exceptional, beautiful and worth sharing.

Later, in the chapter on speeding up your process, you will read about how we learn through our stories. I believe that it's more important to live my story, however it turns out, than to have stayed small. The story, and the names I use, may not matter to you. The teachings do. If they resonate in your heart with truth, beauty and goodness, that is your proof.

Other books have recently arrived using the words 'Christ vibration' and promising that if you read the book, and practice its techniques, you will be lifted into that vibration. I asked Anna and Michael to tell you, dear reader, if that would be true with this book.

Actually, yes. But the way it works is different from how you think. Every time you ponder the meaning of life, the existence of a higher power, or your deepest purpose, you light up. Reading any book that sparks these thoughts/feelings will light you up, even if you disagree with its contents.

To accelerate this enlightenment, ask for help as you read. Yes, these words are empowered as we write them. Yet their power is hidden. As you ask, your feelings and thoughts will light up at the messages of significance to you.

To take it further, if you feel so inspired, start talking to us. As you will read in the sections describing ***The Way Of Alive***™*, we are available for communion as often as you ask and make time for it.*

You are in charge. With your unqualified permission, we will change your life. If your intent is to offer yourself in service, then it is our will that you be helped.

"What are you? A vibration? A collective?" you ask.

Nope. We are distinct personalities. It took time for us to reveal that to Anna Michael Krista. We had to test her first.

Chapter 5

Why Do I Use The Word Christ?

When all is lost, and even the love is gone, would I still trust, and hang on to, my own basic goodness, and to my faith in God?

The Christ *is*.

These precise words came out of my mouth one night with such exquisite, crystalline, divine resonance that I do not doubt them. The word 'Christ' itself rings like pure choral bells when Anna and Michael and I use my whole body to speak it. I love using this word, because it makes me feel joyfully sacred.

It wasn't always this way.

I spent a lot of time on retreat in Peru and learned to love God via ayahuasca ceremonies. You will read more about this later. One night in June, 2013, I lost myself completely in a ceremony. Layer after layer of life as I knew it folded in on itself and disappeared. Finally I myself disappeared. I was aware of only one thing: absolute, pure, divine Love. Actually, I was more than aware of it. I *was* it.

I came out of that journey repeating the word 'Love' over and over again with my hands pressing the word all over my body, and then into the body of a friend lying beside me in the maloka, the name the Peruvians give their circular ceremony house.

I knew then the truth that LOVE IS ALL THERE IS. Everything else is illusion.

I was given this experience because in the weeks and months to come it was the only thing I could hold onto. That, and the fact of my healing.

You will read more about how on June 11, days before this Love journey, I had been joined with a Divine presence. Since then, it had been infusing me with exquisite, active, intelligent Love. Specifically, it was using my hands and other body manipulations to help me stop a vicious chewing addiction that had been destroying me for fifteen years. I was enamoured. Every waking moment I breathed gratitude to this presence, and invited it to continue. Isn't that what we are all seeking? Direct communication and unequivocal guidance from the spirit world? Not to mention a miracle of healing?

A short month later I was scheduled to leave Peru and I felt panicky, knowing that the chance of me fully breaking the cycle of addiction by then was slim. Would the Love go away? How could I carry on the process when back in Canadian culture? Even though I had never heard of such a presence sticking around in the daytime, after the ceremonies were over, as mine was, I still wondered. Was my experience dependent on the medicine? On a retreat lifestyle?

Nope. It is still here, purified. However this hasn't been an easy process. I will attempt to describe the horrific nightmare that followed.

Back in Canada, I stayed in a cabin on some friends' well-loved forest property, while they lived up the hill in the main house. I continued the retreat lifestyle by spending most of my time alone, doing healing practices with this presence, and eating very little. A grapefruit, an avocado, an individual portion of smoked salmon, no more than eight pecans, and six bananas were about it for each day. Maybe a sundried tomato.

I felt fantastic. I was being helped with every aspect of daily life, and experientially learning esoteric healing techniques that were beyond any modality I had ever heard of. In fact, this presence incorporated all of them -- chiropractic, acupuncture, psychoanalysis, shamanism, cranial-sacral, osteopathy, nutrition, yoga and more.

It was starting to speak with my voice. More and more easily English words were coming out, with no medicine and no ceremony. One magical night, alone in the main house lying upside down on the couch with my head on the floor crooked in a position artfully designed to release my neck, I felt pinned down and a forceful voice spoke through me.

"This is Jesus Christ. Your name is Anna."

Wowee!

He told me to set up a website named astraenergy.com and gave me instructions for changing my name. When he finished, I flew to the computer to search domain names. I would have flown across the continent in that moment if he had asked me to.

If I had known the extremes that voice would take me to, I might not have been so eager. The lessons to come were severe; yet I now feel blessed. I learn from them still, and the benefits that I have received since are based on the choices I made then.

My blanket devotion started to be tested, almost right away. After so many weeks of ecstatic results, I was giving this presence full permission to direct me. From being a queen of independence, I was now fully content to submit obediently, every moment, to bodily direction as well as verbal guidance. Bit by bit, these instructions got more outrageous.

For example, this presence started to hint that I shouldn't eat so much.

"It's easy to go without food," my voice said silkily at one point.

He -- a pronoun I used from the start for this presence -- told me a friend was waiting for me, but it was a lie. He asked me to stay in bed all morning, working with prana, even when I knew the dog needed to be walked. Everywhere I followed his lead, he pushed me a little bit further. Pretty soon, I felt like a toy being shaken in a dog's mouth. He did things that the Jesus you imagine would never do.

I guess I'm gullible. I was also scared that the healing process would stop. My chewing issue hadn't stabilized yet, so I went along with his suggestions, treating every abuse as though it was just something to be learned from. My attitude that everything is either good or a lesson kept me going. I felt good, even honoured, despite all evidence to the contrary.

I'm embarrassed to tell you the rest, but Anna and Michael urge me to.

One day, this presence led me to enter a well-prayed-in sweat lodge that was on the property, a part of my friend's shamanic practice. There, on my knees in the dirt, the words, "This is Jesus Christ. I have returned" squeezed majestically out of my body.

The glimmer of possibility teased briefly -- it has to happen to somebody, doesn't it? -- but the weight of disbelief won out. This didn't feel like Jesus. It must be a lower entity capitalizing on my issue with grandiosity, which I must have if this was happening to me.

My disbelief was validated when, after the dramatic declaration, the purported Jesus followed this momentous announcement with, "Far out, eh? Tutti frutti."

I've often used the word 'groovy' in my life, but the words 'tutti frutti' were not part of my vocabulary. The moment was lightened. The ridiculousness of the whole thing made me treat it like a joke.

"What do you do after you learn you are the second coming of Christ?" I asked an imaginary audience back in the cabin, picking up the broom because there was dirt on the floor. "You sweep the floor."

I am now happy to tell you that I am the return of Christ. Don't freak out though. You are too. The return of Christ is an embodiment, which is available to anyone who says, 'Yes.' If it hasn't happened to you already, I'm willing to bet you know at least one person who has had a visitation by Jesus, or who has been told they are Christ. They are reluctant to disclose this to anyone. I'm a guinea pig. I declare, I am an embodied example of the return of Christ. And, as this book will prove to you, I am far from perfect.

In the next days, the trickery accelerated. I fell for it. When I was rudely woken up in the middle of the night and told outrageous things about other planets and Earth's history, my ego thrilled with the thought that I could write a book. When we analyzed my friends and he illumined their darkest sides, I felt glad to know their deep dark secrets. When he told me things about my future that were on the outer limits of possibility, I wanted to believe them. For example, when he said that my former boyfriend and teacher Michael, who had died, was going to reincarnate as my son, I sobbed with gratitude.

When I realized, as I invariably did, that none of these things were true, I meekly said, "Oh, I guess I needed to learn xyz or he wouldn't have done that."

What some might call forgiveness, most would call sheer stupidity.

I had started losing control of my thoughts. This presence became invasive. Strangely enough, through hundreds of journey visitations to the spirit world, I never feared that I would lose the stability of my psyche. Being sensible had always been almost too automatic for me, as it had inhibited me from play and pleasure. Now, for the first time, I felt terrified for my psychological survival.

"I think I'm being possessed by a very high demon," I confided to my friend one night.

"Gee, thanks for bringing it here, to our land," she replied laconically.

Oops.

When I see how I am now called to depend fully on Michael and Anna for my physical survival, I see how invaluable this experience was. If I didn't lose it then, I never will. My sanity, that is.

One morning I finally hit the limit. The voice calling itself Jesus Christ was changing personalities every few minutes, swooshing my thoughts and feelings all over the place. This kind of irreverent playing with me could only be malevolent, I thought.

Had I forgotten that one of my missions was to feel my feelings? Be forewarned, you will get what you ask for. I got it all in a big whammy. Difficult, but that was how they sped my process up.

All the foundations of self I had built during my extensive spiritual journey were shattered. None of my friends had had similar experiences. Despite the extensive grounding that I had done over the years, I had no reference points. By all of this culture's standards, I was insane.

"That's it." I said, desperately scared. "This is finished."

I walked up to my friend's garden and started picking beans.

The presence didn't go away. He would pull at me to get my attention, in a way that feels like being tugged by a strong current. I shut him out. One day he almost forced me to sit down on the sunny moss bank, and poured a vibratory love into and around me.

"Is that all you've got to offer?" I berated him. "Forget it." My analytical mind wanted explanations, but all of his had proved false. If he wasn't going to give me words I could trust, I wasn't having any of it.

"Yes, my healing is sticking around. Thank you for that," I told him. "But no more."

I felt determined to go back to the way I used to be, even if it meant I had to get a day job!

Shut out during the day, his voice starting nagging me in the wee hours, when my vigilance was weak. I could stop him from using my vocal chords, but he could still voice-over my thoughts. For example, one night he said in a smarmy way, "Let's talk. I love relationship issues." This disgusted me. Actually, I felt ashamed that I had fallen for his promises.

It wasn't until I found the wherewithal to say resoundingly, "I am in charge of my mind and you are not allowed in," that he stopped. Take note of that, fellow journeyers in the spirit world ... as well as those who succumb to abuse in the physical world.

I prayed. Oh, how I prayed!

"Dear God, First Source and Universal Center, Creator of pure truth, pure beauty, pure goodness. Help! Only your highest good is allowed to be with me!"

I stressed over how a demon could use the name of Jesus. I had been taught that a sure-fire means of protection is to ask a spirit its name. If it's a demon, it cannot give you one, because they don't truly exist. This I had experienced a lot. It's a way of confronting your fears and taking charge of a scary situation.

"Who are you," I would ask dark images that came to me in journeys. "Are you with God?" was another of my mantras. Invariably this made any horrible imagery disappear. When this entity called himself Christ, I trusted that he really was. Many people have had conversations with Christ in sacred plant medicine ceremonies.

"Aha!" it came to me one day. He was able to not only use Christ's name, but to abuse with it, because we humans have done exactly that! We swear with it, we curse with it. We commit acts of war, murder and horrific 'kindnesses' in the name of Jesus Christ.

So I started qualifying my call to Christ: "I call forth the *true* Jesus of Nazareth, Yeshua ben Joseph, the Jesus who lived on this planet 2000 years ago." I prayed like this dozens of times during each day, often with tobacco, and maintained a constant vigilance against unwanted entry.

By the way, my relationship up until this time had always been with God. That's who I talked to in my heart, wrote to in my journal, and experienced in visions. This Jesus entry was a surprise to me.

In self defence, I stayed busy, working in the garden and processing vegetables up at the main house for my friends.

"If I don't feed this entity with attention," I said to myself, "it will go away." But he hovered. Insidiously, he would slide movements into my now-plain yoga practice with that genius I had so adored. He knew that I lived with the perilous fear that my chewing issue would return and I wouldn't be able to resist it alone, and he seemed to be panting, just waiting for the moment when I would call him back.

Meanwhile I had found one reference point. Tenzin Wangyal Rinpoche, in his book *Healing With Form, Energy And Light,* described how as part of being healed from a chronic illness, his mother had become a new person with a new name. He wrote this as casually as saying that someone poured a cup of tea. I was shocked. I had gone through a horrific experience that possibly was considered normal in Buddhist culture.

In retrospect, I suspect that tests as severe as mine happened often enough in mystery schools and esoteric traditions, but they were so scary that they have been kept secret. Plus, the initiates had close one-on-one contact with a guru who had already been through something similar.

I seemed to be coping, but one thing nagged at me. When things were still pretty good with this presence, he had pinned me down on the bed with my head and arm at a painful angle.

"I, Jesus Christ, warrant my eternal life to you, Anna Christ," it forced out of my throat in a hoarse voice. Then, in response, it forced me to say, "I, Anna Christ, warrant my eternal life to you, Jesus Christ."

A vow in the spirit world, and even a commitment in this one, I took seriously. Even made in this wonky way, against my will, I couldn't discount it. By now I didn't believe his word meant anything, but mine meant something to me. Could I back out of it? What would the consequence of a default be?

One other thing made me extremely ashamed. He had said that we were married, and that my name was Anna Christ. At the time, I talked myself into it being possible. The Bride of Christ is a known concept, isn't it? For centuries, certain orders of nuns have considered themselves married to Christ. Certainly I had lived like an intermittent nun for many years! Plus, on that magnificent night of entry in Peru, I had been told "Your soul is joined now." But where did I stand in the spirit world, now that I had backed out? The level of confusion I felt was overwhelming.

Thankfully, I reached out for help from a shamanic couple I knew. She had channelled various entities for years. I told her I had made a commitment but was too embarrassed to say what it was. There's no way I could tell her about the marriage thing, and the return of Christ experience I could barely admit to myself.

Another point of confusion was that I had been healed in an undeniably brilliant fashion. I felt tempted. Was there a way I could still use that genius to help others?

What a blessing that my shamanic friend had lived through many struggles! She suggested we create a ceremony in which I would state my terms of working together with this entity. He would have to state whether he agreed or not. Because it would be a witnessed event, by my shamanic friends and their spirit guides, he would be bound by his commitment.

Gleaning some hints from Tenzin Wangyal's book, I created my terms and made an offering of flour and water, shaped the size of a finger, to say thanks for the healing. I also made a little stick man to symbolize the entity. If the entity agreed to my terms, I would keep the stick man intact. If not, my friends said, I should burn it and the entity would be gone from my body and my life. If that happened, I intended to formally renounce my vow.

We gathered together, drummed in the four directions and she opened up to her guides. My other shamanic friends in the room did as well. I told 'him' that now was his time to say all the things he had been pushing at me for weeks, that I hadn't allowed in, but he was suspiciously quiet. I asked for his name, as I had been doing all along. The word 'John' came out, and my channelling friend, quite pleased, said he was John the Baptist. I snickered to myself. I knew how easily even this pure and experienced shaman could be fooled. Chances are, he had just meant that he could be anybody, as in 'John Doe.'

I stated my terms. I declared that I and only I was master of my body, heart and mind. I asked him to vow that he would come forth only when I invited him. If I shut him out, at any level, at any time, he could only return when invited. I asked him to vow to assist me, in my goal of helping others, with only pure love, truth, beauty, goodness, and factual accuracy. I demanded that if I brought a male partner into my life, this entity would support him, and us, together. Finally, I declared that he would never interfere with or affect my dog, except through my healing hands. Once she had been behaving strangely, and when I asked it if was him making her that way, he had said, "Yes."

He didn't agree to my terms out loud, yet my friends said that stating them was like creating an armed guard. I wasn't entirely convinced, but decided to let him earn my trust.

"We'll see," I told them. "He's on probation." I left the stick man intact.

Surprisingly, he obeyed, and we lived this truce for months. I still prayed like a mad woman, but gradually started to feel normal again, and opened the door to help others. He had always been truly helpful when it came to other people, and I kept fervently siphoning him through God.

I hung onto two truths. My chewing addiction had been cured, and the Love genius with which I had been helped was indisputable. My experience that 'Love is all there is,' also helped by reassuring me that somewhere behind all this craziness was a pure Divine goodness that knew who I was.

Yet still feeling the need for protection, I considered getting baptized. Even though the traditions in Peru are grounded in Catholicism, the shamans normally work with the spirits of the plants they have relationships with, rather than with Christ. I felt the need of protection in the Christian lineage that I was born into.

I also felt the urge to accept the name of Anna. I truly felt it had been given to me for a good reason; I had never had a meaningful person named Anna in my life, so I hadn't dreamed it up. It helped that with every little church I passed, my eyes were drawn to the cross by this presence with a feeling of serenity. Being witnessed in the official house of God -- even though a typical church service felt mundane in comparison to other rituals and ceremonies I loved -- made sense.

Then one night I had a flashing vision of Jesus. A regal voice, which echoed from my heart, said, "Come to me. I await you." The feeling tone was pure goodness, and my heart leaped with gladness. I asked Him if I should have the minister at my mom's church baptize me, a woman I knew to be sincere and capable. I received an immediate and enthusiastic confirmation, almost as though I heard bells. It took months for it to happen, and she changed the ceremony to a chrismation, which is an anointing with oil for someone who has already been baptized, but the very asking triggered a new set of events in my spiritual life.

A few weeks later, in mid-February, I was walking the dog on a forest road unhappily pondering my eating habits, which had been horribly skewed by eating emotionally for years to compensate for the extreme duress of the chewing addiction. Suddenly "I can help you with that," came out of my mouth.

When I got over my surprise at hearing the voice boldly emerge after so many months, my mind went back to the summer of not eating much, and eating so slowly it took an hour to eat a banana. I resisted the offer emphatically.

"No, thanks, I'm not doing that again."

When the emotion of my resistance had died out, I got curious. Would the guidance be different now?

Naturally I had reflected a gazillion times on my experience of the summer, trying to make sense out of it. Slowly it had dawned on me. Every weird and perverted expression of Jesus had accentuated an unloved part of myself. The holes in my personality -- my neediness -- had been projected in a ruthlessly exaggerated way for my training. The fact that I did everything that was asked, beyond reason, was a test. On one hand, this spirit presence wanted to know how far I was willing to go to follow the will of God. On the other, it was waiting for me to push back.

Anna and Michael are not interested in a puppet or a simple channel for their message and work. For them, that would be like masturbating. Rather, they want a responsible co-creator, one who is actively involved in creating the dream and then living it together with them.

It was another test as well. When all is lost, and even the love is gone, would I still trust, and hang on to, my own basic goodness, and to my faith in God? How stable was I? How much faith in my own experience did I have?

In little ways at first, I allowed this presence to use my voice again. I was still vigilant in screening everything that came through as being from God, and I still asked for a name. When I didn't get one, yet the guidance was truly helpful, I started calling it, "my Friend."

From helping me with food choices -- focusing on the how of eating as much as the what, by the way -- we gravitated toward sessions in which he was teaching me about loving myself. Through stories, discussion, situational analysis and manipulating my thoughts and feelings, mostly while lying on my couch, my Friend resurrected, aerated and cleared leftover unfelt feelings via strange and intense experiences. I will give you an example later.

These 'couch sessions,' as I called them, I wrote down in blog entries while they were still fresh. Friends who have read them say they are confusing, as the teaching often goes in circles, but progressively these sessions built in me an unshakable sense of feeling good, all the way through.

Above my kitchen table, where I write, I have a plaque-mounted print of Jesus, a version painted recently and miraculously by Glenda Green named *The Lamb and The Lion*. I often talk to the image of Jesus, especially liking the way his eyes meet mine wherever I am in the room. I don't mind admitting this because if you are still reading you likely already think I am bonkers.

One memorable day in March, while communing via this picture, my Friend stated unequivocally that He was with, for and of God. He said it in a way that made me feel like bowing in reverence. My gratitude was supreme. After all this time, my tentative trusting of what felt truly, beautifully good was vindicated. What a relief!

During the next visitation, Jesus ordained me to do His work.

I share the embarrassing details of this story to validate that I've been through enough hell to make my story worth telling. There's got to be some teaching in this purification process for everyone! But please know that it doesn't have to be this way for you. In fact, it likely won't. In order to serve you, I had to bear the brunt of some tough challenges. Simply reading, and feeling, the fear I went through will lessen the need for you to go through it from scratch. The perspective and background in this book will give you a big leg up. You will know, if you invite Anna and Michael in, why they are doing what they do. I hadn't a clue.

I am eager to introduce them to you. I will do that by explaining how they unveiled themselves to me.

Chapter 6

Who Are Anna And Michael?

One of my jobs is to help free Christ from the baggage of Christianity.

It has hurt me to use the word Christ. I have alienated Christians who think I am blaspheming, as well as non-Christians who think I am a Jesus freak or on the egotistic edge of insanity. Yet here is my truth.

Michael Christ, according to *The Urantia Book,* a Divine revelation that came through in the early 1900s, is the Creator of this universe who incarnated as Jesus on this planet.

During the first months of my year in jungle isolation in Peru, I stumbled across a free *Urantia* e-book while searching for spiritual e-cards on the Internet. I read the first page of the first chapter and instantly downloaded it to my Kindle. For the next four months I read it at every mealtime.

I was not participating in any medicine journeys, yet I was flying high the whole four months. Truth, beauty and goodness are words used in that book often, and that is exactly what I felt reading it. It's a far-reaching, sophisticated and detailed description of how the world of God works, the unknown history of Earth, plus a full history of the life of Jesus. In my mind, it's what the Bible should be. Its accuracy did not concern me, because I had read many books with information from the spirit world that had the lasting positive effect of opening up my paradigms to what might be possible. This one made me feel exceptionally good.

In April of 2014, while working with a group of people, my Friend came through in the most hilarious way, debunking every sacrosanct belief that many of us free thinkers bet our spiritual lives on and teaching us much simpler truths. I wish I could give you examples, but it was delivered with such a delicate weaving of words and timing that you just had to be there. Each of us collapsed in helpless giggles that lasted well into the next afternoon.

"Who are you?" I asked at the end of the dialogue.

"Michael Christ," He said. And that's who my Friend has been ever since.

"Don't you wonder if you are delusional?" you ask. "You loved this book so much, and you were so wounded, that you projected a fictional 'Michael' because you couldn't believe that you could save yourself?"

Believe me, I have every doubt that you have. The reality is, however, that this presence who guided my every move for six weeks to break my lip-chewing habit is a genius far beyond me. The healing, of myself and others in various ways, is as undeniable as the Love.

"But Michael is an archangel. What do you say about that?"

If you want Him to come to you as an archangel, He will. Or Buddha, or Shiva, or a sacred plant teacher for that matter. Only once was the archangel Michael mentioned in the Bible, in the book of Jude (1:9). Other references, in the Old Testament book of Daniel and in Revelations, were to Michael without the archangel word attached. According to *The Urantia Book*, the statement in Jude should have read, "an archangel of Michael."

Much as I love *The Urantia Book*, I kept asking Michael if it was accurate. For over a year after I was joined, I never got an answer. Finally, it came, and I trust these words because I am given very few facts to hang my hat on. *The Urantia Book*, a set of writings that simply manifested on someone's bedside table, is accurate.

"I still don't trust that you didn't make this whole thing up. Didn't you once have a lover named Michael?"

Yes. He died suddenly in a kayaking accident in 1996.

"Don't you think that screwed you up?"

I have fully felt that fear. And yet the teachings and the feelings I am given are stupendously sane.

What Michael says is that yes, I made this up. And also that it's all true ... Michael Christ is self-existent. Somehow, within the mysterious and marvellous workings of God, there has been this co-creation. Who lifted me while reading *The Urantia Book* such that I loved it so, when not everybody does? Michael tells me He did, to prepare me for what was to come.

As much as I put him on a pedestal, the Michael that I knew in the flesh was not, (and, Anna and Michael say, is not) Christ. The personality that Christ Michael is to me does not resemble his.

Other than my own experience, I have no proof. The degree of accuracy or lunacy in this truth will be revealed by the degree to which I serve others.

"What if I was Chinese, and had never heard of Christ, and could not use the name Michael?"

Michael and Anna are the clearest English translations of their names. They have voiced these names in their pure vibratory form to me, which encapsulates their personalities via the essence of the consonants and vowels involved in these English names. In a similar way, Urantia, the name for our planet, is a vibration that has come to be pronounced differently in every language. The etymology of the word 'earth' states that in old Saxon it was 'ertha,' and in old High German it was 'erda,' words that easily over the ages could have derived from 'urantia.'

More than that, the Christ is a spark of the divine in every person. The form and the name it presents as can be different, or even not verbalized, in another language.

I am happy to talk to anyone with any words they choose. The Divine, the Source, the Mystery, or just plain Love works just fine. I am not interested in converting someone to use my words. However I do ask for the freedom to use the ones that mean the most to me.

One of my jobs is to help free Christ from the baggage of Christianity. The modern Christianity has beautiful aspects, as does any religion, but Christ Michael is far more expansive than any single religion or belief system. Hence the title of this book.

The simple message I am given is that we have a Mother and Father Creator, Anna and Michael Christ -- the great I AM. Both of them are individual personified expressions of the Supreme God. These two presences literally come together to spark each human life, and together they help us 'children' to mature into human gods, just as Jesus, and other rare beings, exemplified. *The Way Of Alive*™ is an exceptional boost to that help.

"Wait a minute. Your name is Anna. Are you saying you are the Mother Creator?"

No. My name is Anna Michael. It's a joined name representing the fact that Anna and Michael joined early for this project. Anna I refer to as 'The Big Anna.' She is self-existent, plus she exists in each person. You may think of Her as the Holy Spirit or the Feminine Christ. *The Urantia Book* refers to Her often as the Mother Spirit. By it's definition (and my experience) She is also the collective mind and the collective unconscious. Many of us have met her as Kali, Gaia, Shakti and Mother Earth ... the Divine Feminine who has kept her treasure hidden and thus has been feared.

"We've all heard these names, but not Anna. Why?"

This being the age of the feminine, Anna is now emerging as a defined personality. I don't understand why we haven't been given that name before, but I am told that it has always existed, and that She is making Herself known because it is time to give Life a new start. More on this later.

This combination of masculine and feminine Christ, in whatever name and form it ends up in you, will reside as a living presence in you to perfect you into a god in a body. This is what we refer to as the Return of Christ. Being fully embodied by Anna and Michael, however, is only the beginning. Your co-creative potential is infinite.

Anna first showed up in my awareness in the summer of 2014, but I see now that She has been with me from the beginning of our joint venture in June of 2013. She has shown Herself to others. For example, She is in Anastasia, the wondrous female depicted in Vladimir Megre's *The Ringing Cedars* book series. There's an American, Katye Clark, who has taken the name of Katye Anna because she shares the teachings of Anna in her books. There are others, I am told.

We don't all have the same teachings, because we are different splinters of Anna, with different jobs to do at different times in different locales.

By the way, do you prefer to use the name Jesus? Or the personality of Buddha? Please keep on doing so. I was given the name Anna in August of 2013, Michael the next April and Krista after that. Why not all at once? They were responding to my choices as I made them. This is another aspect of this journey. You are in charge, and how you manifest your name -- and your god- job -- will be a co-creation.

"Didn't this joining happen in an ayahuasca ceremony? Aren't you concerned that using a plant medicine to access an altered state has deranged your mind?"

No, because I apprenticed with a tradition that has helped people for thousands of years. The ayahuasca medicine does not harm. It helps. It is not addictive nor toxic. In Peru I even gave it to my little dog. When I picked her up an hour or two later, her body was as limp as a wet noodle. This extreme relaxation allowed Anna and Michael to work on her more easily, both via my hands and their spirit helpers. Lately, her vet has admired how loose her muscles are, given her advanced age and the damage to her spinal column of two dog severe dog bites that left her hind legs working at about 80% capacity.

If you feel called to it, I will always recommend judiciously using plant medicines; there are many available species that have been used all over the world for eons. They open a portal for Anna and Michael to speed up your process easily, which is ideal for *The Way Of Alive*™. Other means are available, but likely will require more elapsed time.

For me, the buildup to this joining started years before I worked with any plant medicines. Now, Anna and Michael are *Alive* presences within me every moment of every day without any external substance involved. The medicine simply expedited a critical part of the process.

The work of the shaman in an ayahuasca ceremony, to simplify it, is to access the power of the spirit world to heal others. While a high-calibre shaman is necessary to hold sacred space, I am suggesting that you use the medicine to access the power of Anna and Michael yourselves. With the medicine, you will be much more able to see, feel and physically experience many of the immense and fabulous changes that await you. My experience of this is irrefutable and irreplaceable. You will read stories about this later on, but I don't expect you to believe it via my words only. Go to Peru and experience it yourself. Then, you will know that what I am talking about is possible.

Yet it is not a pre-requisite. Creating a unique expression of Christ is a brand new *Alive* that is possible for anyone who asks for it, gives permission for Anna and Michael to work with them, makes the time, and who dares to say, 'Yes' to devoting their lives to the good of all people. If you don't choose to use plant medicines in the process, Anna and Michael will figure out a different way. Please, do only what you feel deeply called to do.

The personalities of Anna and Michael have unveiled themselves to simplify our approach to spiritual growth. Going straight to Mom and Dad does make sense! It's a relief to be able to relate directly to *who* is behind the Mystery. *How* they do things is unfathomable to me, and infinitely creative. I am attempting in this book to describe my current understanding of what they are offering for this planet, for the life of each human, and for me, but the layers continually unfold. Different versions of our future have been prepared. Which one, or variation thereof, will thrive? It depends on our choices.

Chapter 7

Heralding The Way Of Alive™

Love this life like a new puppy.

"Tell me more about the future," you ask. "What is this purported plan to save the planet?"

W*e see Love gone wrong,* say Anna and Michael. I*n fact, the big problem is what we don't see because it is so dark. Most people. You used to be one of them. We like this problem. Darkness is fertile and creative, like murky, bubbling compost. This is the opportunity of your lifetime. To seek the Light.*

"How do I do that?"

Love this life like a new puppy. Be relentlessly playful, inquisitive, trusting and unfailingly affectionate. That is the highest answer. What, where, when, why and how your planet's problems get fixed is not as important. Not right now. Quite simply, you do not have the skill required. That's where we come in.

Ask Anna Michael Krista. Her healing required someone to be with her 24/7, someone who understood precisely how to tweak her body, mind and heart. Only pure Love has that genius. We are that.

Similarly, your world crisis is bigger than any one person can solve. It requires an extraordinary level of genius, acting in concert through many humans. Love is that.

Most of you don't understand the word Love at all. It's no wonder. You've been held back from feeling us fully. Until recently, this world has been quarantined from the spiritual circuits of pure Love. That Love is intelligent, wise, active energy. Omnipotent, omniscient and omnipresent. It is what Anna Michael Krista described as a living presence inside her, complete with personality. That is who we are.

And that, on a large scale, is what is needed for this planet now.

We created you. We designed you to be vehicles of the pure Love. For many reasons, this did not take place in the regular way. Your planet was orphaned from us many, many years ago. What has happened is one of the most delightful opportunities in our Universe. On one level, we get to remake you. On another, you get to remake yourself. It's a co-creation of Absolute Magnificent design.

This is what we call The Way Of Alive™.

"How do I join up?"

You ask, and you give us permission, over and over and over again. You make time to let us in. We help you. As we earn your trust, we heal and teach you -- body, mind and heart -- more and more. At some point, determined by you, you offer us your life in service to the greater good. Then, bit by bit, as it suits you and our plan, we become a living presence inside you, helping you to re-grow from the ground up. Literally.

Anna Michael Krista's body has been rebuilt. She has basked, 24/7, in the Love of us, completely changing her heart, thinking patterns and soul into a design meant for future generations. We are propagating this experiment to many humans.

We understand this presents some worries. Who wants to be regrown? To learn everything, all over again, like a babe? Who wants to join themselves with the unknown spirit that we are? What about the horrific growing pains that Anna went through to get to this place? Here's the good news. We have upgraded each of you with her experience. This means that your process does not have to be so intense. Yet this path, to be frank, is the biggest adventure you will ever embark on.

You may fear losing your life. Your uniqueness, your feeling that you are you. You won't.

However, to be honest, already you are not only you. You are also us.

I, Anna, Life itself, am the spark that enlivens your flesh. I, Michael, Love everlasting, not only created you, but as your Jesus, I splintered myself on the day of Pentecost and ever since have resided as a spark of Christ inside every human. In addition, the spark of the Supreme God, the Creator of us and all things, entered you as a child. We are a lot more as well, but we simplify these definitions for the purposes of this manifesto.

We three act as one. We are your intuition, your guidance, your inner vision, your higher self and your still small voice. Until now, we have had your safety in mind, of your personality, heart and soul; but not of your body. Basic survival has been up to you. Your ego knows that.

In Anna Michael Krista, we have ignited our spark into a living flame, an undeniable presence sharing her body and loving her every thought and feeling to stimulate her to put Love first into every action. Her prior skills, tendencies, memories, and unique personality are intact.

But now that she is joined, physical survival is not her problem, but our joy. We have her back. Her fleshly concerns are now our own. As our living, breathing, physical child, she is safe. Her part of the agreement is that she is our agent for good.

Yes, we want to work like this with you. Why?

Looking for direct spiritual guidance, in infinite ways, has mushroomed in your society in recent decades. You are asking for closer contact, and this unveiling is partly a loving response to that. It happens to coincide with our plans for a new Way Of Alive on this planet, one that is healthy, happy, hearty and harmonious. Besides that, it's fun. This adventure is supreme. Laugh uproariously, live outrageously, learn voraciously and love foolishly are the four precepts that we live by, and that is what we translate with you into a life of happy giving and meaningfully expressing yourself.

You do not have to be a nun or monk, or give up your home life.

In fact, we love the home and family life. We rank the job of mother and father most highly.

This is where your world has been broken. Your Creator Mom and Dad -- us -- were not around to love you into proper, natural, nourishing behaviour. Even if you had a good childhood, we hereby tell you there is much more to be learned about truly loving, laughing with, teaching, and igniting the divine in your children.

Secondly, we have an ulterior motive. Newly imprinted Divine Christ children are waiting to be born. Yes, 'newly imprinted' implies a brand new breed of human. One who has the full expression of us already implanted in their bodies as babies. What could this be like? One vision we hold is of parents, joined with us in embodied communication, having early telepathic-style conversations with their newborn children, and sharing the tremendous responsibility of nurturing a child with our expansive wisdom.

It is physically possible. Sudden leaps in mammalian evolution have happened many times before on Earth. We declare that this is a good time.

Thirdly, the way your world will be fixed is with our cooperation. Some of you have been working very hard at manifesting from thought. Ever wonder why sometimes it works, and sometimes it doesn't? When we concur with, and enliven, your desires, anything is possible. If we don't, your efforts will boomerang back at you in unplanned ways.

We add that this is good, too. We are all about learning, and about you becoming gods in a body, fully expressing your, and thus our, creative potential. There are multitudinous paths that need to be taken by both of us for this expansive, eternal, long-term vision to happen. Not all of you will be called to work with ***The Way Of Alive***™ *as outlined in this book. We have other plans for you which are equally good. Regardless, each of you, we pray to God the Supreme, will make lots of mistakes on this path. Making mistakes and learning is the only way this plan will evolve.*

Your planet is not fixable by human effort alone. We offer you our genius, our wizardry, our compassion, and our love. At times, when we have your joyful cooperation and it's beneficial for the good of all beings, we will coordinate your efforts concurrently. We might start practising this, for example, in some of your sporting games, or in song, or in healing each other in the way that Anna Michael Krista already described. The choices of how, what, where, and when will always be up to both of us.

By the way, we are in a hurry. Even though we are eternal, and regardless of your choices we will all survive at some level, we have very delightful reasons for renovating this planet that we cannot fully reveal. Not to mention that the lure of co-creating this brand new adventure, never before attempted, is just too much fun.

We do hope you will join us.

"Okay, let's do it. How do we start?"

Chapter 8

Call To Action

Put love first, regardless of what you are doing, and good things will happen.

Just say, 'Yes' to devoting your life to Love.

"Yes. Now, tell me how to do it."

Sorry. No can do. You have to figure it out for yourself.

"What's the point of this book then?"

Honestly, this is not a 'how to' book. It's an inspirational motivator for you to carve your own path. You are unique. No one can tell you what is optimal for you to do in each moment, except your own inner guidance. And even at that, only you, regardless of guidance, can choose the life of being a fully expressed god in a body.

I can't tell you how to do it, how long it will take, who to go to for advice, or what your experience will be. I can only describe to you the way it worked for me, which I am doing as fully and transparently as I can in this book. Once you say, 'Yes,' Anna and Michael will guide you impeccably.

"I have a guide that I already work with. Do I have to give her up?"

No. There are other beings that work as helpers for our loving Creators, but why not go straight to the top? Anna and Michael know the highest beings, in any moment, and the optimal resources to apply to your individual needs. Put yourself in their helpful hands. You cannot see the big picture, the one that includes your loved ones, your full potential, the people that you will affect, the full planetary situation, and more. You are not aware of all the gifts at your disposal, and you don't know for sure the best next thing you can do for humanity.

Put love first, regardless of what you are doing, and good things will happen. Things that you could not have planned, have barely dreamed of, and will everlastingly be grateful for. The miracle of grace works this way. We give up knowing what has to be done, and turn the 'how' over to them. Focus on Love. From there, Anna and Michael will lead you step by step with a perfection that you will only see in retrospect.

Here's a suggestion. Start with a mantra like "I Love My Life." Shift to "I Love Life." Migrate to "I Love." Turn that inside out and say, "I Am Love." Then, take the 'I' out of it and exist only as Love. The more you do this, the more Love will boomerang back, exponentially, to lift you into a happy life, regardless of what it looks like compared to others.

Love like a new puppy, even though life happens. This is the ultimate instruction of this book. All of the other ideas and suggestions are subservient to that.

And please, keep yearning for more. No matter how many years you are on your path, no matter how healthy your relationships become, no matter how in tune you are with your guides and helpers, please don't stop. Follow that little niggling in your heart that whispers, "There's more!"

The Way Of Alive™ teases that niggling by offering you a quantum leap into who you can be. Or, to say the same thing, into re-membering yourself back to your original design. Yet it takes time and attention. You will make changes, and take risks. Mistakes will be created for you to learn from, over and over again as you go deeper. At times, this path will ruthlessly kill things -- including your definition of self -- that you desperately want to hold onto. You may feel deeply disappointed. Glories may be held in abatement until you are ready, or until the time is right for others.

Yet my experience suggests that this adventure is so worthwhile you will keep diving in, and taking huge leaps of faith, even after, and maybe especially after, you fail. Saying, 'Yes,' opens a huge door to the pre-existing spark of God within you that is your essential motivation toward perfection.

Even with that, you have current responsibilities to consider. Family, money, your own sanity. As you go, please, stay in right relation with these things. Your basic goodness will advise you.

Know this. You cannot make a wrong decision. You cannot go faster or slower than you go. You are perfect in every moment. We love you truly, as you are.

The Way of Alive™ embraces infinite methods of embodying I AM. Love is your only rulebook. However, to help you streamline your choices, Anna and Michael ask you two questions.

- *To what degree are you willing to lose your life? To stop thinking, speaking and acting as though you own your life? You don't. You tap into a single life force that flows through all things. Take the 'I' out of your life, ruthlessly, and you will expand into the preciousness of Life Itself, Anna, more easily and rapidly.*
- *How deeply do you love God? Your faith will be tested. The more you trust in the ultimate good of anything, the more you will ground into the basic goodness that you are. These tests will build the foundation required to carry you through the toughest times, and the roots required to flower your highest potential.*

In the following chapters we give you ideas, suggestions, and a lot of stories. If you conscientiously read/listen to these words, while asking for assistance from I AM, your co-creativity will burst forth and your next steps will become clear to you.

You need to jot these ideas down as they arise. Download your *I AM a Creator* workbook, which gives you stimulating questions and space to make notes, and keep it beside you with a pen as you read.

Download your free workbook, *I AM a Creator,*
right now at www.thewayofalive.org.

We thank you. Your adventure in joining with I AM is your gift back to us. Verily, you do not see your impact on us. It is unique, multi-levelled, holographic and sooooo worth sharing. Everything you think, speak and do for your embodiment helps every being in our universe. We share this for you. We also ask that you choose to solidify this sharing in your dimension via y/our beloved Internet.

You are writing your own story.
Tell us yours as you go on the forum at
www.thewayofalive.org.
You are worth sharing!

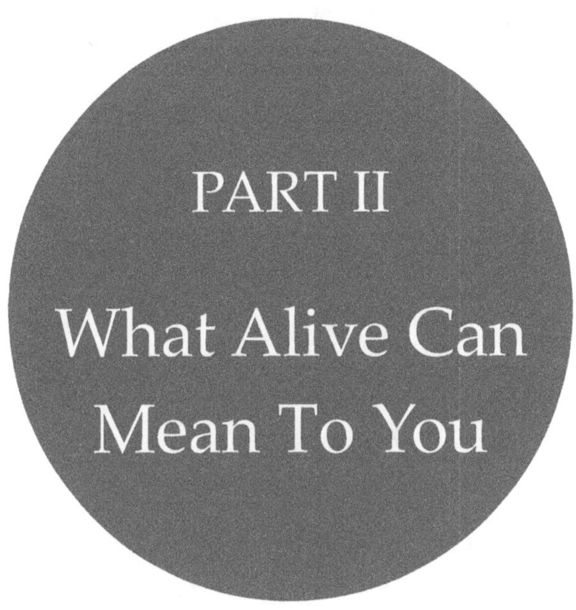

What you are right now, as an average mortal of this realm, is a seed. "Alive" is your root, your growth, your fruit, and your progeny.

Chapter 9

My Story

Is it really possible that each of us, seven billion, are cultivated to be a Christ?

So far, you've read a lot about how my life is now great. It wasn't always that way. My chewing issue was a silent scream so horror-filled, and so consistent, for so many years, that I sense it sent a blaring siren out into the universe. Maybe Anna and Michael just plain got tired of listening to it! Yet I have no regrets. Although I feel sad when I think back on the struggle, I am truly thankful for all the ways I sabotaged my life. They carried me, perfectly, to Anna and Michael.

Whatever 'stuff' you are going through, I firmly believe you are being groomed for your god-job. My life story is not more chosen, or more special, than yours. I have learned that Michael and Anna work with each human being consistently to cultivate the Christ potential in them. Every human can be the return of Christ, especially in recent generations as Anna and Michael have been preparing to come forth. Look back, and you will see their work in your history of synchronicities, repeating intuitions, curious habits and leanings toward a higher power of some kind.

As a trivial example, all through my life, whenever I tried out a new pen to see if it would work, I wrote the word 'because.' It took me years to notice that I even did it. It was a hint, from Michael and Anna, that something significant to that word was on my horizon. I now know why; future books I am to write will be answering 'why' questions about Life Itself.

If you say, 'Yes,' when you are given your god-job the major events in your life will resound with this clarity. What you don't detect on your own, they will, in time, elucidate to you in a life review, the kind you expect to have when you die, when all the threads of your life tie together with perfect sense. They do this because they want you to clean up all the undone aspects of your current life, to make more room for the work they have planned for you.

"Is it really possible that each of us, seven billion, are cultivated to be a Christ?"

Unbelievably, (still, to me), yes. Here's how I think of it. Anna and Michael stack the odds. They want a certain number of people to build up enough confidence to keep saying, 'Yes' to the point of full embodiment, and therefore they nurtured you, and everyone else, as though your life was the most important one of all. Essentially it is, for the job they have planned for you. There's magic in here somewhere that I don't understand, because not everyone will say, 'Yes' and at the same time, everyone who does will have a job crucial to this project. There are also other projects. The most I understand is that Anna and Michael perfectly, in every moment, re-adjust their plans to optimize the choices we make with our free will. There's something going on here with time bending, which I do not even attempt to understand.

I am now going to share with you the events in my life that built up to me joining. You can learn from the stumbles and fumbles I made in my life choices, and either avoid making some of the same mistakes, or maybe dig yourself out of them more easily than I did. It's also a little selfish: sharing my story transparently is a means of letting it go and moving onto something new. Your takeaway point is this: know from my example that you are loved, and have been beautifully nurtured, through each of your trials and joys, for the job they would love you to say, 'Yes' to.

Chapter 9.1

Death On Two Legs

I defended, I denied, I struck back and cried.

I used to chew myself out all the time. Why am I not good enough? There's more to life, I know it. Why don't I feel it? Maybe I should have ... If only ... But ...

I had a fine childhood. No physical deprivation, no physical abuse. Two older brothers and two older sisters who, they say now, doted on me. Parents who loved each other, spoke as one voice and who stayed together for 55 years until my dad passed. We grew up swimming, water skiing, snow skiing, and playing with our friends outside.

Granted, Dad worked and Mom was busy. My eldest brother bullied us. The humour around the dinner table was sarcastic, even hurtful, which I can't figure out now because my folks were so mild-mannered.

You get the picture. Regular dysfunction, but nothing special.

That was the problem. I didn't feel special. I remember one night in particular, as my eight-year-old self was being shunted from one sister's room to another, (neither one of them wanted to share with me), saying, "I'm nothing but a nothing." I still have my diary from those years, in which I scrawled, "I HATE MYSELF," a written expression of how I felt much of the time.

Why?

I now know. An unconscious part of me remembered Love, the way my Mother and Father God loved me. I missed it.

Simple, isn't it.

I was so shy that in Grade 8, after we moved schools, I did not speak a single word to one person for the first two months. This deathly fear of being with people ruled me until my first solo retreat when I was 36 years old!

Let's drop in on my 34-year-old self. I had completed three university degrees, was in my twelfth year doing technical marketing with IBM, and had let go of both a 10-year marriage and a long term affair.

A whisper of an aspiration, to be a writer, had remained safely dead since age eighteen.

I had never been inspired.

Like the tin man in *The Wizard of Oz,* I trudged and clunked my way into and out of other people's ideas of life. My spine was seized up, most of my feelings ended up in my stomach, and I peered out at the world through a headache 24/7.

Sadly, I didn't expect much else.

I had never met 'else' before.

It came to me embodied in a penniless street photographer named Michael who was totally unimpressed with my four-bedroom, four-bathroom house, my 'achievements' at IBM and my impressive golf scores. He catapulted me into my first big death.

I had never met anyone who truly valued life before.

Are you shocked that no one in my circles were following their wildest dreams, living by unpopular values, and acting without compromise? Michael was like this. He created more adventure in one day of his simple life that I had experienced in a decade.

I had never met anyone who was so vibrantly alive.

While working at IBM in Toronto, I used to park across the street from the entrance. Every day, I should have walked an extra fifty meters to cross at the streetlights because a sharp corner made it dangerous to cross the traffic. I didn't. I ran across that street because I craved at least a tiny moment of feeling adventurous in my day.

I was so thirsty and hungry for some kind of meaning in my life when I met Michael that I grasped at him as a saviour. Hopelessly infatuated, I tried every means possible to lure him, catch him, have him, devour him. When he called me out on my childish manipulations, I fiercely defended who I thought I was.

His mother had left his family when he was six years old, and for twenty years he had been working to heal his feminine side, which he also saw as completely missing from our culture. I hadn't even woken up yet. I didn't see the gap between us.

He liked me enough to try to fix me. One by one, he slashed my illusions with the machete of truth. My job was a sham, my marriage had been a lie. I used sex to get love, instead of to give it. My jokes were nothing but cruel sarcasm, my eyes didn't smile. My feelings were frozen. When I tried to placate him, to say what I thought he wanted, he repelled me. He wanted me to be real. I had no idea what that meant.

I defended, I denied, I struck back and cried. What did he know, this strange little man who hadn't even finished high school? He finally rejected me completely, leaving me feeling like a formless puddle of water on the floor waiting to be mopped up or stepped on.

I forever bless him. His adamantine sword loved me to death.

Over the next months, when I wasn't stalking him, I studied his mentors: Carl Jung, Jiddu Krishnamurti, Erich Fromm, and more.

"Gosh darn it," I eventually admitted. "Michael was right."

Slowly, strand by thread, I knit myself a new life. I couldn't have Michael, but I could, and did, take the parts of him that I admired and become them.

I resurrected myself.

Chapter 9.2

Not All Who Wander Are Lost

Freedom, as an ideal, has justified wars.
Yet few people like to live it.

Conversations With God by Neale Donald Walsh was the first book I ever read twice right away. As soon as I finished the last page, I turned back to the first. This book turned God into a guy.

The dead mumblings in the protestant church I grew up in never moved me. The sermons and prayers were never talked about in our house. After the service, the first questions of my siblings and me were, "Can we go out for lunch? Can we get Kentucky Fried Chicken?" To be fair, my mom and dad lived a Christian life. They just didn't talk about it much, taking, I feel now, the high road of exemplifying it instead. For some reason, it never reached my heart.

Conversations With God released me from the dead Father in the Sky. When gushing to my friends about the book, I would say, "And this God guy says ..." this and that.

I was living in a cottage on the ocean in Nova Scotia that had cheap rent because the water was orange with rust. Once I realized my skin never stained after a bath, I loved the place. I spent eight months there writing a book about my experience of Michael because he had ceased to exist on this plane.

We had reconnected six months after he left me crushed. With my defences gone, he became my unofficial teacher. For the first time, I experienced unconditional, consistent, wise, unattached love. I used to call him my vegetarian relationship, because it was all spirit and no meat. We were just friends.

After I had learned from him all I could, (still fantasizing that we might get together now that we were emotionally more on an equal footing), he died suddenly in a kayaking accident, on a Christmas Eve under a full moon.

I had already left my job, sold my house and stopped fruitlessly energizing unsatisfying relationships. I owned only a vehicle and some investments. With Michael gone, I felt a strange contentment. I had known four men, deeply. I had had more love relationships than many women. I was now free to serve.

Where? What? Who? When? How? I had done what everyone said not to do -- stripped my life of everything at once. I was not an IBMer, nor a writer, nor a wife, nor a mother. With no external definitions of self, no external commitments, and a nest egg to fall back on, I had complete freedom.

Freedom, as an ideal, has justified wars. Yet few people like to live it. Essentially, external freedom like this means that no one cares what you do. So how do you decide?

According to teachings I remember hearing from the Buddhist nun Pema Chodron, the answer is to sink into the unknown, rest in it, and wait until the pure light of truth rises up through the muck of conditioned thinking.

It's not at all comfortable. Yet for years, this was the only way I knew to release the jewel of self. Every time I fasted, sitting for hours in one spot, fighting the boredom and saying 'no' to compulsion a million times over, I was gifted.

One night in that cottage I left my life behind. A cute guy in a blue jean jacket, wearing a baseball cap over his curly black hair, jaunted up to me in a dream.

"What's your name?" I asked.

"God," he said casually.

He walked around to my right side, touched a healing into me, bent down and whispered my life's mission into my ear.

Such is the reward of the quest.

Chapter 9.3

Dirty Bare Feet

If I was dropped anywhere on the earth, I wanted to be able to not only survive, but thrive.

The young man might have been blond if he washed his hair. His feet sticking out of tattered army-pant legs were striped with ground-in dirt. He sat as though he didn't have any bones, and his blue eyes piercing my soul were absent of trying. Here was a being at rest.

I was not that.

The lingering image of this child of the earth dangled tantalizingly at the distant edge of who I knew I could be. Every step I took to get there was a hump, an anticipation of insurmountable discomfort that consistently dissipated into the fabrication of fear that it was.

After a fifteen-year hiatus from the wilderness, I sat an entire night outside allowing my childish fears of the bogeyman to abate. Another night I clutchingly walked alone in the woods at midnight under a full moon, only to find the shadows befriending me, the hills hugging me to their bosom, and the water singing me a song of welcome. This ex-IBMer and former fanatic golfer spent three years, off and on, sleeping in a tent, living with ticks, stripping life down to the bare elements, and learning what it would take to survive in the woods with only a knife while at Tom Brown Jr.'s *The Tracker School* in New Jersey.

One of Tom's main instructions was to pursue any experience that pushes your edge. The edge experience itself is a powerful teacher. I took this to heart.

If I was dropped anywhere on the earth, I argued to myself, I wanted to be able to not only survive, but thrive. If I lived every extreme, I would be balanced. After living flat-lined for thirty or so years, my thirst for adventure was insatiable. The relief after my first big death, via Michael, led the charge. Always, no matter what, I would be able to pick up my pieces -- the ones I still wanted -- and re-assemble them into a whole and freer me.

For eight years I chased that edge by living out of my van and re-resurrecting my life regularly. I spent six months letting things go at Pema Chodron's Tibetan Buddhist monastery in Cape Breton; I separated the teachings of Jesus from Christianity while folding laundry at Iona Abbey in Scotland; I learned that work is a privilege to be enjoyed, and to separate it from making money, while cooking at spiritual centers like Salt Spring Yoga Center; and I relaxed into experimental anarchy by hanging out in a shamanic eco-village.

"If I was to die in six months," I would ask myself when deciding what to do next, "what would I rather have done?" My driving motivation came from a phrase I remembered reading that Carl Jung said just before he died. Even though he hadn't done everything he wanted to, he had done the most and the best that he was capable of doing. I chose carefully, and did everything as fully as I was capable of doing.

One day I looked down and was surprised to notice pus oozing from several long-standing bug bites on my dirty shins, and that my feet were cold. I didn't know how long they had been this way. This child of the earth had arrived.

Chapter 9.4

Biting Into Alive

That energy was Life Itself, straining for expression.

For hundreds, perhaps thousands, of nights, I gazed through the mesh of my tent to feed from the mysterious moon and know-it-all stars, and simultaneously anchored my sense of self into the center of the earth. Wherever I happened to be geographically, these were my constants. Dying to self withers the horizontal, temporal attachments to relationship, environments or identities into the nothingness they eventually will be, to make room for this vertical, eternal Self.

Dying is not only necessary on this path, but natural and essential.

If you are like most people, you grasp onto who you think you are because to shatter that illusion is scary. What if there is no 'you' left? I felt scared, and did it anyway. Brave or foolish, either label works.

My goal was to transcend the fear of not knowing what to do next, such that I could rest in the unknown and allow the untainted missives from God to direct my life. To my dismay, the fear never went away. Yes, I had been given a life purpose by 'the God guy' and held it close to my heart. Yet it was a wispy phrase, far beyond what I could ever imagine fulfilling. A dim beacon of potential, it offered no direction on how to live my daily life.

I didn't know then the power of Love.

Living without structure had broken every habit and shaken every pattern of thinking to its core ... except one. It took a long time to get down to one root issue of not feeling good enough. When it had been dispersed in the thoughtless life I had carried on until I met Michael, which I later described as 'death on two legs,' this essential unease hadn't manifested into much. Poor eating habits, shyness and mistakes like having an affair seemed rather common in my world, and I didn't link them to a desperate need to feel seen and valued. This problem turned into a monster only after I pruned these bad habits. The energy that had been driving them simply funnelled into one concentrated, debilitating neurosis.

That energy was Life Itself, straining for expression.

While standing on my head one day at the end of a yoga practice, I noticed that if I moved my jaw a certain way, a little tissue in my mouth ripped that wanted to be free. This made sense. I had been so tongue-tied as a kid, my mouth hadn't grown properly.

I was on retreat then, and spent time forcing myself to sit still rather than to be productive, so that I could value myself for who I was rather than for what I did. This forcing created a gap, because I was not yet who I yearned to be. Working the jaw to free its perverted constraints snuck into my daily life by giving me something to do. Insidiously, it gave me the illusion that I was making progress. How easily curiosity slid into compulsion!

I had no idea that Anna and Michael would have filled that gap in an instant if I had asked them for help with my jumbled thoughts and difficult feelings.

Yes, I had a relationship with God, but it didn't occur to me to pray. Rather, I focused my energies on trying to read the signs, to interpret the messages, to develop my personality through my own intention. An energy rush, a message in a dream, or an encounter with a deer I took as indicators of my spiritual progress.

How many people had I helped? That was for later, when I became a better person. I was on a mission to learn how to love, and didn't feel nearly good enough at it yet.

Over the course of the next fifteen years I nearly chewed myself to death.

It was the great gift of life.

If something like this is what it takes to bring you to God, do it! Suffering is useful. However, it's no longer necessary.

Chapter 9.5

Filling The Gap

I was with you then· I understood· I helped you with that· You did this because we intended that· You did not fail· You have always been with us·

Flash! You meet someone for the first time and recognize them. For one delightful instant, you feel known, seen, valued and understood. Starting from this baseline, you foolishly say things you would never dream of saying to a stranger. Oops! You back off, embarrassed, and revert to the polite, scared, smiley world of 'getting to know you.'

You have just felt God.

You may not fully believe me yet, but I testify that God has been with you every moment of every day of your life. Your every decision has been influenced by God, your every mistake nurtured with love, your every action blessedly enlivened, your every feeling graciously accepted.

I was lifted into this ecstasy of knowing during a sacred plant medicine ceremony shortly after I arrived in Peru the first time. An unbelievably exquisite presence reviewed with me -- in English -- my journey of life, saying, over and over again, "I was with you then. I understood. I helped you with that. You did this because we intended that. You did not fail. You have always been with us."

Is it any wonder I decided to die to the life I had been living, and to offer myself again?

For six years I had been living one life. After my urge to change myself from the outside via nomadic adventures had spent itself, (and despite a former commitment to never own a house again), I tried a new approach to fixing my chewing problem. I bought a little house and challenged myself to break out of my pattern of self-containment and risk the adventure of long-term relationships. As a reflection of my independent nature, I lived off grid, and started helping others to do the same by offering a solar system design and installation service.

I liked it, and I was good at it, but not good enough to stop chewing. Disappointingly, this latest strategy -- that of keeping busy, right livelihood and right relations -- didn't get underneath the entrenched complex that, however psychological in origin, had built up a physical momentum so strong that neither I, nor any of the dozens of healers I went to, could stop.

When I resisted the bite, the tension would build, feeling like nails driving into my mouth. I would struggle to count to ten before biting down to break the tension. Within seconds, the pulling would shift to the next spot. The cycle consumed me, often for twenty hours a day. If I was lucky, in a month I might get one or two free days. My life had become a fight for sheer survival, psychologically at first and then, as my organs and bodily chemistry were ground down over time, physically.

A gynaecologist urgently wanted to operate on an ovarian cyst four to five centimeters in diameter near my left ovary. While she was in there, she said, she would very likely find she would have to do a hysterectomy.

Cutting out the mere symptom of the cyst would be useless. I knew the plant medicines by then. In a ten-day tropical retreat, untold layers of compounded tensions had bolted uncontrollably out of my mouth and body like a volcano. That gave me hope that the medicine would help me dig out the roots of my monster. In May, 2010, I went to Peru.

Within three weeks I had decided to close my business, rent my house and become a shamanic apprentice.

I was still chewing, but God had spoken to me. During the day, for about three weeks, a translucent shimmering light surrounded me. A feeling of pure and simple goodness permeated me all the way through, far beyond what I had ever imagined feeling good could be. A divine presence which surprised me with it's delightful personality regularly visited me in ceremony. For the first time in fifteen years of experimenting I felt rooted, and took this as a sign to pursue the medicine path.

Because of my prior experience with dying to self, disassembling my life was easy. I finally felt comfortable enough in the world that I knew I could recreate money. I kissed and said good-bye to my satisfying role as 'The Solar Lady,' in town. My mom and siblings, well trained by this point, were unsurprised and wished me well. My little dog and I set up house in a screened-in, thatched-roof hut in the jungle. Within a month, an angel had descended upon me in ceremony. Putting a tiara on my forehead, she said, "God is pleased with you."

Still I chewed.

Over the next three years of immersion I loved God for hours many, many nights. The more you love God, the more God loves you, they say, but I only believed it after I saw, felt and exalted in miraculous physical, emotional, psychological and spiritual healings night after night after night.

Still I chewed.

"Sunday I worked the jaw so hard I decided I was insane," I had written in my journal in 1998. "It is completely unjustifiable, from any rational basis, to bring onto myself such excruciating pain."

Thirteen years later, I wrote, "All day and night Tuesday were brutal, jaw-wise. Literally, I couldn't sleep. Yesterday it kept up till about 4 p.m., and today it's going strong.

My story had not only gotten boring, it was dangerous. The word 'cancer' danced in my shadow. Heart attack or organ failure felt imminent. My digestive system was destroyed from eating despite, and worse yet because of, extreme tension.

By contrast, I peppered my journals outrageously with large-printed words such as, 'THANK YOU GOD,' 'WOW,' 'MIRACULOUS,' or 'UNBELIEVABLE ANOTHER WOW.'

They just kept healing me.

They never gave up.

Sear this in, dear reader. No matter how messed up you are, your Mother and Father Creators love you unconditionally and forever. Their love of your life is eternally and infinitely yours. You just have to choose it.

One wondrous night, June 11, 2013, amidst what I heard and felt as choirs of tender angelic beings in an event that seemed to be trumpeted throughout the universe, I was handed a golden orb and told, "This is your soul. You are joined now."

A living presence of divine origin settled in me. From that moment, this loving presence actively directed my movements with a beyond-genius precision to stop the biting. (It took six weeks, and I had a couple of relapses over the next two months, but it happened. The cycle was broken.)

On June 18, I was enveloped by a being of pure radiance and experienced that this was my future Self.

Miracles like these are available to you.

In this book you will learn how simple it is to acknowledge, admit and embody this perfect inner guru yourself -- without the suffering and extremes that I went to.

Simple, but not necessarily easy. My chewing addiction is gone, but the lessons are tricky as only a maestro of perfection can devise, and sometimes even severe. Nonetheless, I still say to Anna and Michael, "Have at it. Do what you will with me." My quest was worth it. I have been freed.

Chapter 10

Who Would You Become?

To learn is to move along the gradient of consciousness of who we already are. To join while we are still in this body is a quantum leap along that gradient.

"It sounds to me like you've just had the classic Christian experience of being saved," you remark.

I have a hard time accepting that, for two reasons. One is that such phrasing has always had an oily feeling to me. Desperate people suddenly become fanatical about converting others. It seems like they've simply displaced their extreme issue with a different form of escape. I confess that this is possible with me, except for the second reason. I am still me, and, believe me, there are still parts of me I need to improve. But more importantly, I share my body and sense of self with a living presence of goodness who is different from me.

Before I was joined, even though I had surrendered my life to service (albeit imperfectly), and tried to purify my inner guidance, it was a lot of detective work.

For example, on my first solo retreat the following statement echoed hauntingly in my half-asleep mind one morning.

"The myths that lead the moment are the guardians of the flowers."

I felt thrilled. For golden crumbs like these I strained, for years before and years after, diligently recording every scrap of a message I could glean from my dreams and rare mystical (if I allowed myself to interpret them that way) events in my daytime life. This was one of the first clear, direct statements I had been given. I clasped onto it like a jewel, as evidence that my struggles would bear fruit someday.

What did the statement mean? I had no idea. How to apply it in my daily life? I could only guess. The very pondering took me places I needed to go, but it took years.

"That's the problem I have deciphering my spiritual guidance," you interject. "It can be vague and obscure, fragmented or just a nudge. I wonder if I am making it up, or if it's my shadow, leading me astray."

How would you like a personal guru, one that knows you intimately, better even than you know yourself? One who speaks to you in grammatically correct sentences? One who is literally present with you, helping you in ways perfectly devised for you alone?

"It sounds too good to be true."

This is the where the wizardry of Anna and Michael come in. They are part of your unconscious as well as your conscious self. They will tweak you in ways that are not necessary for me, and vice versa. Your tests, trials and joys will be perfectly devised for you alone.

They know your imprint, your original design, and precisely how you will serve them and others brilliantly. They understand psychology, the body-mind connection, the spiritual truths you operate with, where you have succeeded and where you have fallen down.

"Yikes! You mean they see my every thought and feeling, nasty or not?"

Honestly, there's no need to worry. They already do. They love you regardless of who you believe you are in any given moment.

They are your perfect medicine, operating on your body, mind, heart, soul and imprint simultaneously. We each have a prism through which we operate in the world; they know yours, and will come to you as your best friends: casual, funny, kind, and someone you can relate to completely.

On a few rare occasions, I have been blessed with experiences of them as they are, without filtering themselves through my prism. Absolute Magnificence are the only words I can use. Pure Love, although they each personify it differently. I wish that experience for you too. I've found that it's a two-way street. The more you trust them, the more they will bless you.

"I'm not sure I want to lose myself like that. It sounds to me like you are being manipulated."

Yup. Michael and Anna manipulate my body, thoughts and feelings. I have given them full permission to share 'me.' I admit, it does take some getting used to. But it's worth it, because in return I share them. It's Love, through and through and through.

Here's the way I see it. Every person is a combination of genetically formed flesh, the force of Life, the force of Love, plus a unique personality that chooses. That 'you' is also, temporarily, the habits, patterns and body shape that you have grooved over a lifetime of reacting to others and the environment around you.

Yet your unique personality is also not just 'you.' It is created by, and still a spark of, the wondrous personality of God, who I believe is the Supreme Creator of numerous universes. I contend that everything we are is, always was and always will be fully joined with God, Michael and Anna and that this seeming split is only a veil between our unconscious and conscious selves.

"When you put it like that, the idea that I can lose myself by joining with who I already am is rather funny."

To learn is to move along the gradient of consciousness of who we already are. To join while we are still in this body is a quantum leap along that gradient. We used to wait until we died to do this.

"You say you are still you, but you've changed your name completely. Why did you do that?"

It was my choice. When the idea first occurred to me to change my name legally, I felt ecstatic. Anna and Michael then said, "Why do that? It's not needed." I backed off. I had always liked the name my mom gave me, and didn't want her to feel hurt. Plus it's a lot of niggling paperwork. But slowly an inner knowing matured in me that my calling is to merge my identity with theirs. It won't be yours. In the people that have joined so far, some of them have been given a new name, neither Anna nor Michael, and some haven't. It's not up to me. Plus, if you are given a name, you will choose what to do with it.

"If I'm already part of them, do I need you? Can I join with them on my own, in my own way?"

Absolutely. I wish heartily for a group of us to start living together as a tribe here in Southern British Columbia, and expect other tribes will start up elsewhere, but I will not coerce you. Anna and Michael are very strict about this. If they want you on this project, *The Way Of Alive*™, they will call you. Whether you are near me or not is immaterial. More than that, they don't even want everyone to say, 'Yes.' They have many other projects in the works; be free to accept one of those. However, even if you don't feel called to this one, please continue reading. The stories, suggestions and new information coming up will be useful to you.

"It still seems so radical. To have another presence in my own mind, talking to me, sounds darn scary. Plus, if we are all joined to them, do we start hearing each other? If I was hearing a dozen voices at once, I'd go crazy!"

Telepathy is in the plan, but not until we are mature enough to handle it. It's enough, in the beginning, to hear their voice in your mind and get used to working with them in that way. Once you are gently nurtured into that aspect of their teaching, others will unfold.

Verily, there are divine rules that everyone in the spirit world must follow. One of them is to never violate your personality. Your free will is sacrosanct. You will feel deeply bonded to others who join with us, but your unique personality will always be intact. Expanded, yes. Celebrated, always. Respected, forever.

"I'm still not sure. I need more information."

Chapter 11

What To Expect

We use every tool, dark and light, to help you grow. When you say, 'Yes' and invite us in, you are inviting strong lessons.

Consider that the purpose of Life is to learn. That is why time exists. In the world of the eternal, all is already known. The adventure is in the change and growth that time provides.

Right. We created you, each human, with god potential. We wanted to learn from you, as you learn how to develop that potential. However, never have you been completely on your own. We have been teaching you via Anna Christ, Life Itself.

"Life is difficult. Suffering is unbearable. Why did you do that?"

Suffering is a catalyst for learning. It plunges you into your depths of character, calling you to live by your deepest truths and highest values. Mistakes are inevitable and highly prized, from our perspective, because we both learn from them.

"Where is your compassion? The idea that you deliberately create -- even enjoy -- suffering is outrageous!"

You don't think we feel the physical pain, right? Wrong. Anna is Life Itself. She is experiencing everything you do. Every single thought, word and action is a very lived experience in all dimensions of our Universe.

"So why the pain?"

We created the garden of Life and you decide how to grow in it. You are players writing your own script. When are you going to free us from your suffering? That is our persistent question. You have all the resources at your disposal to develop as gods. Yes, you need our help. Pardon us, but we have told you before. Ask, and ye shall receive.

"Have we not been asking?"

In recent years, yes. It's like a tidal wave. And here we are, announcing that you no longer need to learn via physical suffering. The point of suffering it that it takes you into depths of feeling that you otherwise avoid. Choose to feel your feelings, and the enactment of a play to bring you to that feeling state is not necessary.

"A friend of mine has participated in many Sundance ceremonies, dancing for four days straight in the high heat of summer with no food or water. But her reason for doing so was different. She says that by actively choosing to suffer physically like that, she is offloading the involuntary suffering of others. Is that what you are talking about?"

Volitional choosing of life's lessons without involving the flesh is our preferred method, but the prayer aspect of that kind of ceremony is highly valued.

You turn to me and ask, "Have you suffered since you've been joined?"

Not physically, and I live with very little drama in my relationships. But oh, those lessons are tricky! It's a wild ride that would freak many people out.

"Why do you keep asking for more?"

Because in the midst of the most devastating realizations, shameful humiliations, unconventional body manipulations, false stories and painful feelings, I feel Anna and Michael's undying motivation of Love. Plus, I see results. I feel good about myself, all the way through. I am happy, tail-waggingly, much of the time. My body feels healthy. I am able to serve others, without feeling scared the way I used to. I am funnier than I ever used to be.

In other words, Anna and Michael fill my gaps.

We do love, all the time. We use every tool, dark and light, to help you grow. When you say, 'Yes' and invite us in, you are inviting strong lessons.

Learning from them is not like reading a book. There is no part, sub-sections and classifications into a, b, c, and d. They teach in circles, in layers, and by influencing thought, word and action simultaneously. To focus on a body movement without involving a mind meditation would be a waste, for example. They will use all available resources in any given moment freshly, wisely and creatively so that they can work with you anytime and anywhere. Every single moment that you open to them, they will be hinting, pulling, guiding or downright taking you over to make a point.

Nonetheless, I will attempt to categorize some of their teaching methods.

- Stories are their primary teaching tool. Only by living out a story can the feelings of a lesson be felt bone-deep. The tricky part is, you think the story is real until you learn the lesson. Prepare to feel like the stuffing has been punched out of you when the truth is revealed. Then, I am sure you will say, "Thank you," especially since it will have taken less time than if you were stumbling around like I was for almost twenty years.

- They also use stories to test your faith. Suppose they tell you that someone will be healed by your touch. How much you believe it will help to build your god-job. You may not heal that person, but they will know whether you have the required faith, and build your next lesson from there.
- They give you something, and then test you to see how much you retain. For example, they led me in my food choices for a few months, and then, once they figured I ought to have learned the principles, they started leading me astray, waiting for me to say, "I know better than what you are telling me." Frustrating? Yes, but part of growing up.
- Along the same lines, they play you like a fish. Suppose I ask for guidance on a certain situation, and they give me a direct answer. If I doubt, or question, they enliven another idea or two or three, like letting out slack, to see how much I will buy into. When I start to doubt the new information, they tighten back up, restricting my options until I rebel. Then, they sit back and wait, never letting go of that safety line, for me to figure out the best strategy to take ... which often goes back to their first answer. This dance brings my fears to light so that I can work with them.
- They enliven your needs and desires. Suppose your desire to serve others is confused with your need to feel wanted, or recognized, as mine has. They will fulfil both at the same time. Because of their pres-

ence, I am safe to take these risks -- to serve others even though I make mistakes. They fill any gaps that I create. Afterwards, the feeling of failure, that I could have done more or better or differently, to put it frankly, sucks. Yet it makes me learn. Because of the perfection of all things that I feel at the time, I trust that others have gotten precisely the help they needed, even if it was in the form of a trigger. Anna and Michael tell me this is true, and many people have thanked me after the fact.

- They layer your lessons. They may lead you down a garden path, charging a certain idea or thinking with a feeling of *Alive*, so much so that you know it's going to work out perfectly. When it doesn't, you realize the process was the perfection and the results don't matter. Along the way, you learned much more than you could have imagined. No matter how disappointing it might have felt at the time, months later you find yourself still gratefully learning from the experience.
- They bust myths. One way they do this is by modifying my thoughts, playing with my judgements of good and bad to streamline my thinking. For example, the basic question we incessantly ask, "What am I meant to be doing right now?" is one we grossly complicate. We are meant to serve others, and ourselves, in any way we can, in whatever way we can think of in any given situation. There is no better, best, or preferred time or place or approach to do this. It is far

more important that we try. How did they grind this truth into me? By shifting my feelings about whether doing this or that was good or bad so much that it didn't matter. Getting rid of the judging process frees up more room for simple service.

- They teach the integration of body, mind and spirit from the inside out. We have spent oodles of time lying in bed as they lead my attention to move prana through my body, clearing out emotional and energetic tension blocks, which trains me to help others in a similar way and develops single-pointed concentration at the same time. In addition to physical manipulation, they lead me via feelings of goodness to express beauty through the physical form in many ways: by uplifting my deportment, encouraging my circumspection, guiding me to care for my sexuality, upgrading my etiquette, migrating me toward a much more feminine way of dressing, and reinforcing basic and consistent habits of cleanliness.
- They will also ask you to give them time, alone and at rest, for them to upgrade your body. Plant medicine ceremonies, which we will talk more about later, are their preferred vehicle for doing this, especially at first. Those medicinal substances relax your body enough for them to do major work quickly. The bonus is, you can usually watch and feel them doing this, although I doubt you will understand what they do. That is why I call them wizards.

- They are with you, 24/7. They know you, through and through, and they like you anyway. Their intimate friendship has a way of naturally eroding any negative patterning that you have grooved in your life. When they do point something out, they often use a humour that is so gentle and understanding that just being seen is a relief that heals. In fact, fun is built into every moment, although sometimes it takes me a while to acknowledge it! Just in the way that everything about you is exposed, tenderly cared for and forgiven when you die, this is a similar process.
- They exaggerate feelings in order to make a point. I attribute my persistent happiness to them, because it sticks even in situations that used to make me feel uncomfortable. In this way, they are teaching me the truth that every bit of us is loved, all the way through, all the time. They also super-charge my feelings to bait me, as in thrusting forward the thought, "Oh, I need to do this right now!" to see if I will take the bait. If I have an habitual reaction in a trivial situation, like, "Oh, that doesn't matter," they may make me take a deep dive into feelings of fear to uproot a malignant thought pattern. More and more I catch them doing this, which reveals another level of teaching: where do my thoughts and feelings come from? At another level, where do these thoughts and feelings live? They want us to probe into these essential truths.

- They joke with me, especially when I am stuck in thinking that I am a bad person. For example, I caught myself admiring a shape I was making in a yoga pose in a mirror one day. After I chastised myself for being vain, Michael said, "It was me who was admiring you." Many of these things that we habitually beat ourselves up for, such as a scattered mind, easily getting distracted, wanting others to like us, being forgetful, rushing, over-thinking about food or other pleasures, are completely exonerated. We are human! Most of these are simply foibles, designed into us, endearing reminders that we are not yet perfect gods. They are not crippling faults to endlessly focus on.
- When we serve others, Anna and Michael come to the forefront and directly use my hands and voice as required. This helps me to learn, and after the fact we discuss my perceptions of the person and the advice we gave so that I can learn to take more responsibility next time. Debriefings like these with Anna and Michael can end up in arguments, debates, and corrections. I love them!

How many of these techniques they will use with you, I cannot predict. I often feel like a guinea pig. Yet the truth, beauty and goodness I feel from them is so strong it's hard for me to believe they make mistakes.

We do. We admit that we are learning along with you. We encourage our joint mistakes. We do this deliberately. The results of our work together will make it easier for others. Plus, they will learn that it's safe to make mistakes.

For the record, according to *The Urantia Book,* ours is one of the few life-experiment planets. This means that in *The Way of Alive*™, the world is yours to co-create. Keep your ***I AM a Creator*** Workbook close beside you in the next section, to jot down your explosion of ideas as you read my suggestions on how you can co-create your process of joining with them.

Get it here, and come say, "Hi," on our forum.
Let's learn together for free!

www.thewayofalive.org

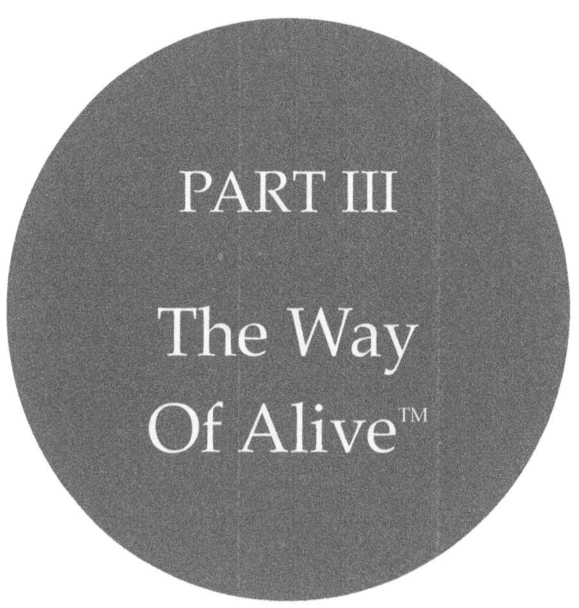

Uncertainty with security is the essence of the Paradise adventure ...

-The Urantia book, 111:7.1

Chapter 12

Ask And Give Permission

Allow your own experience to prove us right or wrong.

'T*he' Way Of Alive* is an incorrect designation of how this work actually proceeds. There is only *'Your' Way of Alive*. With Anna and Michael, every moment is new and there are no rules. However I make one strong suggestion. Experiment with using their names. Your choice paves the way for them to work with you. Do you feel called to do this work?

"At this point, I only want some more information."

Great. Ask them. Call them by name, as you read this book, and you will be surprised.

"And then?"

If, when and as you choose, give them permission to work with you. To the degree that your heart is sincere, whatever guidance you are receiving right now will be up-stepped dramatically.

"Does that mean the entire method you are offering is, 'Just say 'Yes?''

We do live for the moment you say, 'Yes.' Then, we plan for your future life as a living god in a body. Your eternal future is something like that anyway. But, as you choose, it changes.

Yet that is only the beginning.

Let us try to describe what the process might look like for you. Suppose you have a family, a job, and other responsibilities. That's one frame through which we work. Another is that you are single, and could carve out a time period for this to begin. Either way, we do suggest that you have a family for your support system. By this, we mean a tribe. A group of people who understand your motive, your ideals, and are doing something similar. At the beginning, you may have to use the forum at The Way Of Alive™ website for this.

Anna Michael has been developed in a certain way. Your entry will be different. Regardless, your beginning will need a lot of good, simple, profound, living advice. You will glean a lot of that from the following stories and suggestions.

Most importantly, whatever you are doing, start communing with us. We are already talking with you via signs, symbols, synchronicities, emotions, visions and dreams. Once you deliberately ask us for help, by name, and give us permission to work with you toward embodiment, we can make this more specific. We want to speak with you in your language, both in your mind and using your voice, and to teach you via sharing your body. Anna Michael will now give you ideas on how to encourage this based on how it works for her. Your way may not be the same. It may not happen the moment you give permission, or even after you say you want to be joined, because we have to feel you are ready too. We have everything perfectly timed. If there's a need, we will accelerate this process.

Above all, prepare to be silly.

Years ago, I lived with a woman who would spontaneously converse in an incomprehensible language with her spirit helpers. In play, while drumming around the medicine wheel, my other friend and I occasionally allowed gibberish to come out of our mouths in childlike imitation. I never expected it to develop the way it has.

Much later, alone in my little hut in Peru, I started doing more of this. It felt fun to let loose in this way. On my walks, I would memorize and sing indigenous Shipibo songs, but I also left time for free sounding. My jaw was used to making all sorts of twisted gyrations via my chewing, and eventually I discovered that this created some pretty cool sounds. The effect of ayahuasca opened up my vocal range, and at times an invisible force started charging this practice with power, such that I felt like I was being sung. Then what sounded like words started coming out, with rhythms. I started to be able to sing intuitively in the maloka during ceremonies. Soon, when the shaman came to sing to me I found I could sing along with him or her, even though their songs were always worded freshly. It was a practice of suspending judgement, criticism and expectation in order to simply follow what the moment was calling for.

—❧—

This took time. Remember I was there, in almost complete isolation, for over a year. If you really want to start speaking with them via your own voice, I suggest you build this practice into your daily life. For example, a friend of mine sings call-and-response gibberish with his daughter in the bathtub every night.

Try to release yourself from expectations. One man who recently joined is getting his thinking turbo-charged, because that is part of his god-job. He doesn't hear the distinct voice of Anna and Michael inside his head the way I do yet. In the same way that you cannot compare your path to another's, even though you cycle through similar lessons, we cannot compare our processes of embodiment.

Anna and Michael first started communicating with me via the body. That is where I needed them the most, to stop myself from my chewing addiction. Suppose you use your hands in your livelihood, be it as a healer or a carpenter. To invite Anna and Michael in, start hesitating before you move. Ask them, in your mind, if there is a more efficient way. Play with shaking your hands loose and letting your fingers be moved. When you touch someone, imagine the long spiritual fingers of Anna and Michael going inches further into their body to manipulate healing. Give them an extra moment or two to do this, and ask them when they are finished. When you are lying quietly, invite them to move an isolated body part, maybe a wounded one, such as your wrist or your head, in a healing way. Practice sensing their encouragement, and follow it, no matter how subtle it seems. Take the time, and invite them to play with you.

To open to verbal communication, pretend you are talking to them. If you have a habit of talking to yourself out loud, or conversing with your pet, focus on charging that with the possibility that Anna and Michael are the ones answering you. During meditation, or while in a half asleep state, listen for their voices in your mind and start asking questions.

"What do I do when I'm obsessing about someone or a certain situation? It's impossible to empty my mind, or start a new conversation."

Talk to the person directly in your mind. Say everything you want to say. Vent to Anna and Michael! At the bottom of your distress is a deep caring. Anna and Michael will, as loving parents do, automatically use your strong feelings to ameliorate the situation without you having to control it. No one will be adversely affected.

All feelings are a gift to them that they, to describe it simply, spread around for the good of all. Even anger, hatred, jealousy and other emotions, when felt purely, are vibrations that lift others. Give your difficult feelings to Anna and Michael, specifically using words and a sincere heart, to avoid verbally dumping on the person(s) you are obsessing about next time you see them, or, worse yet, stuffing those feelings down until they come out sideways. A tangential effect is that Anna and Michael will replace your donated feelings with feelings of goodness, perhaps in a better way than you expect.

For example, last summer I decided to start working by donation. A client named Randy came along, (no real names are used in this book), and although he was likable and a gifted musician, he was a total sponge. While he expressed some gratitude, he did take for granted that he would be fed, understood, held sacred, and catered to. He was also a slob, which irritated me enormously, and I had to nag him like a mother, which I did not like.

Verbally, I responded with my higher self, but my lower self was outraged. "What do I do with this?" I vented to Anna and Michael.

The answer was that since he wasn't paying me cash, and I performed good work, there was a void. I needed payment, and Anna and Michael said they would fill the gap. They have, in ways much better than cash. Nowadays I feel good about the work I perform regardless of payment, and I love that freedom.

They also refused to let me finish angry thoughts like, "He should have ..." or vengeful thoughts like "Karma will get him." Literally I was prevented from continuing those thoughts. *Just let us take care of him,* they voiced over what would have been the end of my sentence. *We'll take care of you, too.*

"I have another question. What about those sneaky little ugly thoughts, the ones I don't even like to admit are mine?"

Each time you notice one, ask for the mind of Anna, or Michael. Or both of them. Make it a mantra, as in, "I ask for the mind of Anna Christ." Or create your own mantras, like "I AM you are Love," and switch them up. When out for my daily walks I sing each syllable of mantras like these in rhythm with each step.

I AM is an incredibly powerful Word of God. After you join, more and then most of your words will become equally powerful. This started for me way back, when I took a solo mushroom journey. I was thinking about my loved ones, and sounding their names. But when it came to saying, "My sister," I couldn't get the word 'sister' out. In that state of body/mind/heart integration, it was like the pathway from my heart to my mouth was choked with old stories, jam-packed with unfelt feelings. For fifteen to twenty minutes, I worked on verbalizing that word alone. It came out muddy, stuck, twisted, from my stomach, from my restless leg, with a pout, with resistance, with full anger, then sadness and, finally, with crystal pure clarity. I had healed my relationship with myself in regards to that aspect of my life. More freedom. I could now wish either of my sisters well with a clear heart.

Please, I encourage you. Create situations where you have the freedom to do this verbal play. Start prefacing your name with I AM and see what happens. As your relationship with yourself changes, your words will resound like a bell, not only to the people around you, but out into the universe of all living beings. This alone helps others enormously.

At some point, you will likely feel an extra charge to your words when you don't expect it. One thing I am slowly understanding is when my words are charged with Anna and Michael, I need fewer of them. What might have been a hopeful platitude, such as, "trust yourself," can become a statement of truth that resonates into both your core and the core of the person you speaking to.

It's the same with your body. As you give them permission and time, Anna and Michael will upgrade it with palpable Love vibrations. Your body then will be able to shoot those vibrations into others with a simple touch. Laying a hand on a shoulder, looking into a person's eyes, and asking, "How are you feeling?" with pure resonance can be as therapeutic as a full healing session.

"I have a concern about talking out loud when nobody's there, or encouraging the voices in my head. How will I stop from going crazy?"

Good question. Once you have asked for Anna and Michael's help, and given them permission to work with you, you will need faith in both their benevolence and your own good sense. As I have mentioned, Anna and Michael will trick you in order to teach you. The voice in your head may tell you to do something, and you may end up eating humble pie. How do you know which voice to trust? You will figure this out over time. You are safe to play, and to make mistakes, when you are with them. I will share with you some techniques I still use. When they give me information, or tell me a story, I ask questions like, "Is this true, beautiful and good? Is it Absolutely true, beautiful and good? Is this the highest teaching? Is this true, or is this a lesson?"

"I've actually had some experience with this, but my words are stronger, like "Don't give me that crap. How gullible do you think I am? How conscionable is this instruction? Make it good, or I'm not going to listen."

Pushing back is good.

In addition, be careful how you phrase the information or teachings you are receiving when sharing with others. When you receive guidance or instruction, you can fall into a power trap of telling others what they have to do or how they have to feel. Although any mistake along these lines will, once you are joined, be a lesson that's good for all, I caution you to reign yourself in. You can use your knowledge insidiously, with the best possible intention. A young woman recently told me that her new boyfriend had told her he had dreamed about her when he was a very young man. He had been waiting for her for years. Imagine how this compliment swayed her heart.

"If it is destined to be," she asked me, "Should I go along with it?"

My experience is that destiny is fluid. Chances are, he had a dream of a woman who was perfect. She showed up and fit the bill. With the best of intentions he decided to tell her this, but it confused her choice. It's powerful, the idea that the spirit world wants us to do something. It's best to take their input as an opinion only. It's all a testing ground, grooming you for pure co-creation. The power of your free will is sacrosanct, a gift from God that cannot be violated unless you choose, or fail to choose; not even by Anna and Michael. It is your free will that they are counting on for this experimental adventure.

"I only want to do God's will," one woman told me plaintively. What happens, though, if you don't know what God's will is? Rather than spending a lot of time futzing around trying to figure that out, I suggest you take action, put a stake in the ground, and trust that God, or Michael and Anna, will respond perfectly to your decision. Another approach is to trust that as soon as you voice the desire to do God's will, you are, automatically, doing it when you do what feels good. Not just what feels pleasurable, or blissful, but what roots you into the goodness that you are.

"I'm here for a purpose, and I wish I knew what it was," another gentleman said to me. Yes, God has a job for you. However, to avoid waiting for it to magically materialize, simply serve others in any way you can. Experiment with random acts of kindness, for example, or seclude yourself on a retreat. Avoid drifting. Anything you do, with the intention of making it congruent with your god-job, will get you there.

"I appreciate your suggestions, all of them. But I'm confused. I've already got a relationship with Archangel Michael, whose voice sounds very true."

We are ready to say that we are Archangel Michael. Does that make you feel better?

"Only if it's true."

It isn't. We have filled everyone's minds with different spirit forms because that served our purpose. This has changed. This revelation tells you the simple truth.

"As soon as any of us says there's a single truth, we start arguing."

Exactly. Anna Michael Krista has asked us if you could discuss your Divine, your Source, or whatever word/feeling you relate to as your divine guide, as though they are similar to us, but different. They are not. They are we are us. Whenever you pray, you reach your Creator Mother and Father. What you receive, in terms of a visitation, a feeling of presence, suggestions, or urges, comes from us.

Yes, we do dispatch various orders of planetary helpers who are invisible to act for us. Archangel Gabriel is one of those. We also use guardian angels and a host of other orders, depending on the situation and on what you expect. We fill whatever door you open for us.

We cannot expect that you will believe these words simply because Anna Michael Krista wrote them. When you experience them through your own meditations, you will. You may even hear them through her voice. Who is Anna Michael Krista? She is us. When you decide to join, the voice that will speak to you is us. There are others, but we will use them sparingly and identify them when we do. Meanwhile, we acknowledge that the mass conflict over 'who is right' is our creation. What we are saying is that we are your Creator Parents. Simply that. You can talk to us directly, and we will answer as us.

Experience will prove that the straightforward description of the hierarchical nature of beings in this universe and in the master universe, as presented in 'The Urantia Book', is true. Let us add one thing. This is a life experiment planet. Our description in 'The Urantia Book' was completely accurate when we wrote it, almost a century ago. Now, we have changed some rules to allow your planet to be saved. Again, we encourage you to not simply believe everything we say. Give us time and attention, using some of the following ideas, and allow your own experience to prove us right or wrong.

Chapter 13

Make Time And Attention

Because surviving in this culture has splintered you into pieces, you need to bring yourself back together.

Chapter 13.1

Why?

Unless you are already able to put Love first, behind every thought, word and action in your day, you will need to carve out time to do this.

To embody I AM, Anna and Michael will help flower your sensitive nature. This will take time and attention. "Maybe not. I'm pretty sensitive."

I believe you. Most people on their spiritual path are driven by their reactions to our current insensitive culture. The good news is that the new culture will be one in which your sensitivities are nurtured and celebrated, especially the unique ones that become your gifts to others. But right now, my guess is that you hide, numb or are tortured by your sensitivities. I certainly was.

Most likely, you operate on several levels at the same time. There's the part of you that moves you through the day, the part of you that gets the job done, the part of you that your friends see, and the part of you that you hide like a cherished treasure. You may think of this last one as the part you will never let get hurt again.

"To name a few!"

Being god in a body requires the integration of all those parts.

"How do I do that?"

You carve out specific retreats, or adventures. Because surviving in this culture has splintered you into pieces, you need to bring yourself back together. Here's how I started.

When I first left IBM, I ended up renting a remote farmhouse in Cape Breton for four winter months. I was deathly scared of being alone, and that is one of the reasons why I went.

I grabbed together as many projects as I could, to make sure I could fill the time: a guitar and lesson book, my camera and darkroom equipment, cookbooks, books to read, journals, and yoga manuals.

It took me a good four weeks to land. By that I mean that one by one, each of those activities felt empty. I kept coming back to, "Why am I here? Not for this." Eventually I uncovered the root of my essential passion: to fix myself. To forgive myself for having an affair when I was married, and heal the split between my inner and outer selves that caused it. To love myself, even though Michael didn't love me in the romantic way I wanted him to. To find rapture and to love life, from the inside out, without any of the external gimmicks of our society.

I had read about vision quests, and done bits of meditation. What I needed to do, I felt, was to sit with myself, to squirm with the discomfort of who I was until it went away. Ever since high school, I had avoided looking at myself in mirrors. Now it was time to face myself. I set a straight-backed chair in front of a full-length mirror, and with vicious determination told myself that I was going to look at myself until the person looking back at me was beautiful.

I did this for hours every day. Five, ten, sometimes twenty. At times I felt so ugly, so ashamed, I had to forcibly turn my head with my hands to look myself in the eye.

It took three months, but it happened. One day I simply looked at myself and spontaneously laughed at who I saw. She was beautiful.

There was no fanfare after that, no dramatic spiritual moment. I went for a final walk the day I left, and while crossing a bridge over a creek I spat into the water and watched myself float away.

"Was that all?" you ask.

I wondered the same thing. Was it worth it?

Within a few days, while walking down a city street, I noticed some people coming toward me on the sidewalk. I didn't cross the street to avoid them. Huh? It took several moments to realize ... that's what I always used to do! Now I didn't even hesitate to look someone in the eye, because I had already fully accepted, when they looked at me, all of the selves they were going to see.

I treasure the memory of this, my first self-created solo retreat. It was foundational, setting me up with the courage to pursue the lonely nomadic path I felt driven to choose. I was no longer afraid of myself.

It was perfect, for me at that time. Yet ... it could have been shorter, if only I had been able to directly ask for help from Anna and Michael.

Oh, how I had perused the environment for such a thing. One day, while on a walk by a stream, I noticed a yellow leaf had detached itself from where it had clung, lifeless, to a tree about twenty-five feet away. Floating on the breeze, it seemed to be dancing toward me. I put out my hand with an inner jest. No, it couldn't be. But yes, it was! The wind carried it this way, and that way, and then right into my waiting hand.

It was a miracle. I clung to this moment for months as a recognition that someone, somewhere, was seeing and feeling my pain. "Thank you!" I said to an amorphous Universe.

Validation? Yes. Direction? Spiritual guidance? No. The most I could glean from it was, "Keep floundering. You are getting somewhere."

"That whole retreat doesn't sound like much fun."

It was gruelling. Sitting in front of that mirror, restraining every impulse to ferret out the false ones, denying myself the pleasure of food, entertainment, and even yoga to avoid using it as an escape, and trying to force thrills into my walks when I really just felt ordinary.

"And you want me to do this?"

Do it with Anna and Michael, and they will rev up the fun factor.

"Why do it at all?"

If you want to turn yourself inside out, to externalize the precious inner you that you've learned to put aside, you have to prune your habitual self, and to reveal -- and revel in -- who you truly are.

"I've done a lot of weekend workshops to do just that. I've sat a 10-day meditation retreat, and it did wonders for me. Those are the kinds of things that work with my schedule."

Sorry. Those things will work, a bit. You will unveil parts of yourself, slowly. What Anna and Michael require is devoted and creative attention, with open spaces for them to work their magic. Any structured agenda will not allow for this. Unless you are already able to put Love first, behind every thought, word and action in your day, you will need to carve out time to do this.

"I don't have the time ... I can't take the time off work ..."

Do you want to be healthy, happy and hearty? Do you want to skillfully serve others, in a way that's far beyond your current capacity, and help save the world at the same time?

Do you want to feel so bursting with purpose and feelings of being useful that you jump out of bed in the morning and laugh out loud in the shower?

"Yes, but ... to be honest, I'm scared. What if I can't do it? What if I'm not worth it? What if I fail?"

You can't. Effort and decision are always rewarded.

I can vouch for that. It may not be in the way you imagine, but it will happen. Here's another story for you.

Remember the dream I wrote about, in which 'the God guy' healed me on my right side and told me my life's purpose? I didn't intend to disclose what that purpose was, because it's a treasure that I hold sacred. I've learned the hard way that exposing a treasure too soon, to the wrong person, is dangerous. If they dangle the least bit of doubt, it can leap into my raw places that haven't been matured yet. Best to hold these rare flowers close until they have come to full fruition.

Anna and Michael tell me that this one has, although I hadn't thought of it this way. What I'm doing in this book is asking each of you to commune with your Creators directly, so that you will have direct access to all you need to know about the creation, meaning and purpose of life. About the Love they intended you to be. Almost twenty years ago, this is what 'the God guy' told me to do. He said, "Make sure people don't forget the Divine Memories."

Honoured, I was. Divinely blessed. But ... what could I do to achieve such an obscure instruction? So much has been written, so many creation stories have surfaced, what more could be said? In terms of visions, automatic writing or having access to the Akashic records, I didn't have any of those gifts. Would I become a hermit living in the forest poring over piles of ancient textbooks? I was at a loss to know how to let this beautiful purpose direct my life.

Yet I did, just by hanging it like a carrot at the forefront of all my choices.

"You must have been desperate for a purpose."

I was. I hadn't had children, which automatically gives a person purpose, at least for 20 years or so. I had freed myself from all external obligations. What was I to do with my life? "May I make sure people don't forget the Divine Memories," became my persistent prayer. Yet there was no road between what I was doing and that promise to God.

In March of 2000, I wrote in my journal, "It's hard having such a nebulous job as the Divine Memories. But I won't give up. I *am* working on them as I speak." Only now, in 2015, is the road to that job clear.

So here's the deal. If you've ever had a flutter in your imagination that you have a divine purpose, a feeling like you are supposed to be where you are but you don't know why, a far-flung crazy dream of indeterminable source, a spoken phrase in a sleepy state that moved you beyond measure, but you couldn't make head nor tail out of it, or a specific instruction like mine that you've discounted over time, you can depend on it being true.

You each have one of these god-jobs. We guarantee it. We want you to ask us what it is. Please, take the time to listen to us speak. We've been doing so for centuries. All it takes is a sincere heart, and your effort to commune with us. Mostly, all we can get across are obscure signs, symbols, visions, messages and bursts of good feelings to lead your way. Even though it's easier now that the quarantine is over, developing straightforward communication like Anna Michael Krista's takes time and attention.

Chapter 13.2

Why Not?

I waited nine years to have a child. How did I lose sight of how important my kids are to me?

I challenge you. Do it faster than I did.

However, I can't guarantee you will. What I did was perfectly designed -- i.e. long and gruelling -- to help me share with you how to speed up your process. I'm about to do that. But if it doesn't work that way, please forgive us. Whatever happens will prove, in time, to be the best thing for developing your offering to others.

Let's start with your essential motivation. You won't get far without totally freeing this.

"I don't need to. I'm fired up! I want to embody I AM. I want to serve. I want to help others. Let's go!"

Okay. Devote the next three months to getting started.

"I wish I could. I would, but I have my job/family to consider ... I would, if I had the money ... I would, but so-and-so wouldn't like me to be away that long."

But. If. Should. Catch your inner dialogue. Underneath these statements is fear.

Consider Sarah's situation.

Sarah had an enviable life. Two children in primary school whom she cherishes. A rewarding career as a psychologist. A husband who is a medical doctor. What could be wrong?

In a consultation, she told me she felt the call to please God more.

Knowing her family consideration, I suggested that she carve out four days alone, distraction free, to talk to God, to find out how to do that.

"I don't do anything without the kids," she said.

Commendable, right?

Not always. The best thing she can do for her kids, we offered, is to take time out to allow her speeding mind to slow down to the point where it's integrated with her emotional body, and ideally her physical body, and then to cultivate a clearer communication with God.

But valuing her mothering instinct, I suggested that alternatively she cut back on her psychology practice.

"We need the money," she said.

I probed further. Why should she feel afraid when both she and her husband have been working at high-paying jobs for years?

"My husband expects me to contribute fully," she said in a small voice.

It was time for the two of them to re-visit their marital relations, our Mother Anna suggested gently.

We dug deeper into Sarah's fears, and got down to a big one.

"I've had this fear that rules me," she confessed, "that one of my children will die soon."

Mother Anna prompted me to tell her that this is a natural aspect of a mother's love.

"Your fear has merit," we said.

Unexpectedly, Sarah burst into uncontrollable weeping. She was in such a state that it was ten minutes before I felt comfortable asking her why she was crying.

"Because you've just told me that one of my children will die," she whispered. She had interpreted my statement, "Your fear has merit," to mean that her fear would come true.

I told her that, Mother Anna says in my mind.

I got it. Sarah needed to reset her values, so Anna stimulated her thoughts along this wrong path. Creating this story triggered the deep feelings necessary to get her to realize her life needed reconstruction. Ethically, Anna was able to do this because Sarah had given us permission to help her.

After that, it was easy for Sarah to find ways to reduce her psychology practice, only for a few years, to give her children the love they need.

"I'll start by just keeping the clients I really enjoy working with," she said. "I waited nine years to have a child. How did I lose sight of how important my kids are to me?"

Let's say Sarah doesn't cut back. She's asked God how she can do more, she's been shown how, and she retracts. What might happen?

An illness. A disease. A tragedy. A disaster.

A wake-up call from God.

Think about it. What if you were told you were to die in six months?

"I would figure out what was most important to me, and do it."

No doubt about it, desperation works. Consider war, volcanic eruptions, tsunamis and other severely testing events. Anna and Michael do not desire them, they tell me, but they will use them to shake people into finding and living their highest values. Developing character through trials is as old as the Book of Job.

Wouldn't you rather learn via Love, laughing along the way, enjoying it as a fantastic adventure?

Just say, 'Yes' and you will.

"There have always been people who make time volitionally," you challenge us. "Hermits, nuns, monks. Living in a cave is not my idea of *Alive*."

It can be, for some people. We stand on the shoulders of the people who have done this. But living in seclusion is not what Anna and Michael are calling us to do now. Their direction is for us to live fully on this planet, enjoying all the benefits of play, sensation, pleasure, adventure, creation and more. The physical body is to be used, and these features of human life are to be shared.

"I'm convinced. I'm ready to devote time and attention to personal communion with I AM. How do I do this?"

Chapter 13.3

Principles

They will pounce, when the moment is right, to do whatever it takes to develop your needed skills and talents.

The simple answer to the "How?" question is: "Just ask."

Your process of figuring this out is part of creating your relationship with I AM, and part of co-creating your god-job. Yet I can offer some basic principles to guide your way.

In essence, it's this: create quality time to commune alone with your Creator Mother and Father.

"Can you be more specific?"

I recommend that you create an adventure that excites you. Something you've never done before, related somehow to your far-off dream of the wildest and happiest purpose that you can imagine for yourself. Something beyond your comfort zone.

If you are used to being alone, you may choose a service retreat, like volunteering at a spiritual center, or an adventure retreat like hiking The Santiago Way. If you resist being alone, you may choose a mountain cabin or a solo canoe trip. I still leapfrog between these two: a solo retreat to find out who I am without anyone else around, followed by an intensely communal life in order to practice bringing my strengthened inner self to others.

In the next sections I give you ideas on solo retreats, service retreats, adventure retreats, feeling adventures and a lead into the ultimate retreat, the family adventure.

Whatever you choose, your retreat needs a defined beginning and an end. That way, not only do you get into gear and avoid drifting, but Anna and Michael can gear up their spirit resources to work with you. In fact, once you decide to do something, and are ready to design it, create a little ritual to tell them, and to ask for their help right away. Something as simple as writing down your ideas and smudging them, or as full-fledged as a pipe ceremony or private dance celebration; anything like that to demonstrate your commitment will be great. Of course they are always aware of what you are doing, but emphasizing to them that you are serious, and inviting their assistance, will open up the lines of communication and trigger co-creativity.

In the design process, keep your radar out for any opportunities that come your way. Once I started entertaining the idea of going to Scotland, years ago, Scottish people and printed material kept popping up until I said, 'Yes.' Is there one opportunity that grabs you, that seems completely unrealistic? Just say 'Yes,' and let the logistics sort themselves out later. They will. I can't tell you how many times I've been ecstatic after I've done that.

What are your strengths, and where do you need encouragement? Preset some parameters before you go. If uncontrolled eating is an issue for you, plan some fasting. My first time ever fasting for an entire day, I watched five hours of *Star Trek* on TV. Not ideal, but at least I didn't eat. When I went to a cabin in the Yukon for three months, I didn't take a calendar or a clock, because I wanted to naturalize my rhythms. Solo canoe trips challenged me to make every decision, when normally I defer to the leadership of others.

Breaking your habits is frustrating, but if you stick with it, your programming has no choice but to change. It's a process of dying to who you think you are, however you won't be able to do the full job yourself. Your ego's survival instincts are too strong. Don't worry. Anna and Michael have endlessly creative ways of finishing the job for you. Ha ha. Relax, though. In the long run, they will fill your gaps with wizard-like intelligence and the directed action of Love. More on that later.

You may need to empty fully, like I did in front of a mirror in Cape Breton, but another excellent option is to practice creativity, like writing, drawing, music or gardening. Ask for co-creativity, because then you are practicing being a god in a body.

Above all, build in time to not just slow down, but to stop. Your body, I guarantee you, needs not only repair time but upgrading. You do not know how exhausted you are. Lots of rest time will not only slough off layers of underlying fatigue and purge toxins, but give the spark of God in your heart a chance to leap to the forefront. Resting the mind is required before you can free its creative juices.

Physical activity -- simple basic tasks like chopping wood, carrying water or just plain walking -- is great. Unhurried yet purposeful movement steadies the mind because there is no room for analysis or chatter to take over. Releasing the mind from agendas and letting it wander allows emotions to pop through in ways that your busy life doesn't allow.

Spaciousness in your agenda is an absolute requirement. Anna and Michael are fresh. They will pounce, when the moment is right, to do whatever it takes to develop your needed skills and talents. You do not know when that will be, and cannot prepare for it. Remember, your whole purpose is to develop your relationship with them. Yes, you will start talking to them in your mind and with your feelings. Looking for signs of their communication will start to preoccupy you. Once it starts to flow, you need to be mobile in your mind, body and feelings.

Be prepared for the unknown. Their Love will surprise you, delight you, and challenge you into right relation with yourself, them and your natural environment. To free the caring person that you are, they will develop your feelings, especially the uncomfortable ones like fear, sadness, anger and hatred. That is, they will make them bigger in order for you to feel them fully. Just a little something to look forward to.

Take care to design something into your retreat that will challenge your ability to think independently. As you embody I AM, you will be asked to question every societal more with which you have been ingrained. Why you do what you do, in every moment, will be highlighted at some point. Use this time to call yourself to your highest personal truth, beauty and goodness, regardless of what other people might think. Go off grid, for example, so that every habit will have to be re-created. Experiment, allow yourself to be weird. It's a process of aligning yourself with your God-given nature, rather than the current culture, in order to lay the foundation for your work creating the new world. Learn to be strong in who you are, because you will end up clashing with the old ways.

Now, suppose you have children and are not able to get away for long enough. Here is our suggestion. Use your situation as your ongoing adventure. This is a supreme challenge. The constraints you consciously live with will be the tools Anna and Michael use to teach and build your character. Love what you do, as you are doing it, and dedicate it to your children. This is your job as a parent, they tell me.

It will be helpful, nonetheless, to design specific adventures within your situation. For example, take a month and go with your kids to help people in a hospice, hospital, or community project. Build in sharing and reflection time for all of you. Use your vacation to go to that cabin in the woods with an empty agenda. Create experiences with your kids that challenge and develop the full range of everyone's emotions, and then spend time sharing your experiences with the intention of learning from each other. Chronologically, they are closer to their Divine Parents than you are, and have much to teach you.

Whatever it is, ask for assistance and it will flower. Our mandate is to create divine families. You will get all the support you need.

As you read the following ideas, suggestions and stories, take notes. Your creativity will be flowing. If you haven't already done so, download your ***I AM a Creator*** Workbook from www.thewayofalive.org and print it out. Put it in a 3-ring binder and keep it close at hand. Then, share your ideas on the forum, also at **www.thewayofalive.org**.

Chapter 13.4

Solo Retreats

How far can I possibly go toward the highest truth, while staying sane?

My biggest fear was to be alone. To stop that fear from strangling my life, I created the winter retreat in Cape Breton. Wow! What a relief.

It wasn't long before I cherished and protected my time alone like a sacred jewel. While there, if I had one phone call scheduled in a given week I felt constrained, burdened, and relieved when it was over. When I think back to my IBM days, working 40-60 hours a week, adding in chores and relationships and struggling to do yoga for half an hour before bed, not to mention my chronic back and neck pain for a decade in my twenties, it's blatantly obvious why we die young. We are never taught how to live sustainably in the body. And I didn't even have kids!

During those three months, I thought I was preparing for a vision quest. I practiced fasting, staying up all night, even staying up all night outside, so that I would be able to endure the four days sitting in an eight-foot circle under all weather conditions. Little did I know that I was in the throes of an extremely deep and productive quest, largely because I created it myself. I did several 'formal' vision quests after that, and frankly they were a let-down. The "shoulds" and "supposed tos" of other people just didn't work for me.

Similarly, I spent six months sitting four hours a day in a Buddhist monastery, expanded to ten hours a day during a seven-week winter retreat. Although the communal aspects of that experience taught me much, their timed meditation sessions didn't hold a candle to my self-motivated mirror experience in Cape Breton. In fact, during that winter retreat we had a guest teacher come in to facilitate a ten-minute eye-gazing exercise.

"I learned more from that than from ten years of meditation," commented the oldest nun in the place.

I didn't intend to live nomadically for eight years the way that I ended up doing after I left IBM. It's just that the reward of such deep inner changes, personality growth, and progressive freedom from my old selves were worth a mint compared to the cost to my wholeness of making a salary. Much of this I attribute to my solo retreats.

The bravest and most disheartening one I will use as a teaching story, highlighting in bold the messages for you to take away.

I was sitting in a Tim Horton's coffee shop pondering my state of uncertainty. I had squeezed all the adventure I could out of living in my van for the winter in Whitehorse, and had been wondering for two or three weeks what my next move would be. A woman I had met, a loving and wise spiritual teacher, had helped form a consortium of people to resurrect the local hot springs into a healing oasis. She had asked me to join the group, and after sitting with the uncertainty of not knowing for a couple of weeks, I had just turned her down. It didn't feel like the right time.

My date square eaten, I toyed with my tea. Without warning, a distinct voice came from my heart.

"Go out to a cabin for April, May and June."

Startled, I waited for more. When it didn't come I allowed this instruction to slowly integrate into my being. Wow! English words reverberating a detailed message with clear meaning? How stupendous! I wasn't going to turn my back on that one ... even though it would mean letting go of a storytelling festival I had been planning on attending.

I started talking it up. To everyone I met, even snap acquaintances, I put out a feeler.

"I'm looking for a remote cabin to stay in for April, May and June. Do you know of one?"

Sure, the Universe would support me, especially after giving me that instruction. But I had to **do my bit** by putting the thought into words, spreading them like foo-foo dust and **not controlling the result.**

"I know of one," said my friend John Hatch slowly. "It was rebuilt by a friend of mine in the 1980s. The birds will serenade you all day and night. But it's pretty far out there."

It's important to **follow up with every opportunity**. I just said, 'Yes.'

John and I made a van trip down past Teslin to check in with the owner of the cabin, a First Nations man. The cabin was at the mouth of the Big Salmon river, on a popular canoe route. But with winter road closures, I would be some 60 kilometers from another human being until the ice went out, which turned out to be the first week of June. It was March and still at least 20 degrees Celsius below zero every night. I just had time to get organized, charter a plane to fly in with my gear before the ice got too soft to land on the Big Salmon Lake.

"Last time I was there, the windows were broken," drawled the owner, looking at me speculatively. "You will need to put up plastic. And you will have to bring in a wood stove. The one that's there is shot."

Building a cabin is a 'thing' in the Yukon, a challenge commonly embraced by the adventure-loving northerners. But being remote, they are left open for use by hunters and explorers, who, if they follow the normal code of ethics, leave it better than they find it. Not always does this happen.

By this time, I had spent years, off and on, at the Tom Brown school, cultivating my appetite for 'the edge experience.' I had **taken many risks**, always trusting my inner barometer when it said, as it did now, "This is doable. Be extremely careful, and you will be fine."

This didn't mean that I wouldn't make mistakes.

Back in Whitehorse, John Hatch generously helped me make careful lists of food and equipment I would need. Again, with everyone I met, I told them what I was doing.

"What do you need?" they invariably said.

John had a toboggan, someone I freshly met offered me snow shoes, and another friend miraculously loaned me his satellite phone, which, it being 1999, could only be used if a jet was soaring overhead.

"They'll come and get you in an emergency," he said. "But they will get mad if you use it without being almost dead. One fellow I know did that and they charged him $20,000!"

Everything I needed filtered in, after I had taken those initial steps. Expressing my wonder and gratitude to John, he explained this:

"Lots people come up here and say they are going to do things. You are **one of the few who will**. People here respect that."

My target date to leave was March 31st. No way would I fly out on April fool's day! Before that, my friend Carl took me up in his plane so that we could at least see the cabin.

Green spruce trees and white snow is what you see from the air in a Yukon winter. Add to that three brown dots -- the cabin, a food cache, and a back shed. All almost buried in six feet of snow. Gulp.

A bigger gulp came on the day I landed on the ice, as the plane was flying away.

There I was. Alone.

How I wish I had Michael and Anna with me then! Yes, my feelers were out for any expression of spirit. But the idea that a loving personality could help me assess situations and make optimal decisions? Keep me company, laugh with me, crazily love me down to my toenails? Warn me of severe danger?

The highest level of guidance I was looking for was a flowering of my own intuition. To that end, I had brought no distractions with me. Only one book of Buddhist prayers. No journal, no pen. No camera. No fishing equipment, no musical instrument, no drawing pad. It was to be just me, myself and my environment. Whatever I needed I would have to source from within. Yes, it would be dull, but my idea was that the enforced emptiness would stimulate ... something. Whatever it was that I was lacking would eventually erupt and burst me into a new level of loving life. I just had to wait it out.

I still thought I had to do it all myself.

Enforced emptiness is great, and one reason I so strongly advocate solo retreats. However, without knowing what to fill it with, it can be dangerous, like when I started the chewing addiction. Even if emptiness is productive, it's a darn slow, grinding process.

Anna and Michael will fill the gaps with Love. When you create your retreat, ask for this, look for it and feel grateful for it. You will be filled with good ... in a myriad of forms. And what does this goodness do? It dissolves the crap.

I worked hard. You don't have to. Not for things that don't matter.

For example, they would have suggested just the right balance of equipment to bring to afford me a sensitive, fun, fulfilling, entertaining, challenging adventure. They wouldn't have focused on the crap the way that I did -- on the things I felt missing in me. What did that focus create? A strengthened feeling of something missing. They would have targeted the lessons and the skill development that I needed the most, using all the resources of the environment in fun and creative ways. I would have come out of there laughing.

Do you ever think about how spiritual you would be if you had the time and money? If you didn't have this or that commitment? If you had access to the right teachers or friends?

Not being privy to precisely why that mysterious voice in my heart had instructed me to go to a cabin, my fantasy was that I would somehow spend time at that cabin discovering, exploring and embracing the details and wonder of nature. As per some of Tom Brown's teachings, expectations gleaned from field guides, I reckoned, would obscure the spontaneous teachings that plants and animals had to offer. I just had to cut off external influence, immerse myself in the environment, and a deep connection to an inner source of detailed wisdom would naturally arise.

Gaining access to spiritual information is one reason why Tibetan monks spend 40 years meditating. Why did I think it could happen in a few short months? Premonition, perhaps, for the leaps I am suggesting you can achieve today. But likely just plain naivety.

Don't forget about how you felt making those decisions on what to bring, Anna interrupts me as I write.

I think back. My basic question while planning was, "**How far can I possibly go toward the highest truth, while staying sane?**" Each decision I made felt good. Adventurous but safe.

Then why didn't it turn out that way? She prompts.

The first three weeks I feverishly spent cutting firewood, standing deadwood I luckily found in a nearby swamp. Once I had sawed, hauled via toboggan and stacked enough firewood to assure my physical survival, I started to look up, every now and again, at the spectacular scenery around me. I couldn't stop being busy right away, you see. I was scared of having nothing to do.

One day while bending over a fallen tree I felt a start. Not quite a jolt, but a moment of alignment. Almost of its own accord, my bottom sat down in the snow and I heaved a big sigh. I had finally arrived. That is, my mind had slowed down to the point of landing in my body, and my heart had synchronized with the environment.

We live in a state of fight-or-flight, a carry-over from the days when physical survival was paramount. Even without a job or responsibilities, I was full of it. We have no idea how tightly wound up our bodies are. We worry incessantly about avoiding toxins and bad food, and we are constantly looking for a miracle supplement or elixir that will help us sustain our crazy lifestyles without the single biggest healer -- rest, on all levels. Mental, emotional, physical and spiritual. Another word for this is contentment. The feeling of being loved, all the way through, will do this, as you make time for it.

Sitting there in the snow, I felt a glimmer of hope. "Maybe I will find ease here."

I didn't.

My chewing problem had started a few years back. Before going to the cabin I had had four blessed months of relief from it. I thought it was gone, until I started planning this cabin adventure. One wrong move, one missing piece of equipment, and I would be dead. My fears arose. I started to chew again.

"It'll be all right once I get out there," I thought. "When I have time to work on it."

Work on it, I did. Not exclusively, but either doing it, or trying to stop doing it, did end up ruling my life, both at the cabin and for the next 14 years.

That's why I felt like a failure.

You did not fail, Anna says.

Why not?

You tell me.

Okay, let's go over some of the really great benefits of that experience.

Even though the jaw kept me tense, I still felt a wondrous expansion being away from people. When I'm with people, I put up barriers, and I bet you do too. They are instinctive, from having to survive, first physically and now emotionally, in our broken culture. Do you know what I mean?

"Yes. Even when I'm with my dearest loved ones, a certain part of me is on guard."

Something I never consciously felt until I was alone for long enough was that my very being-ness could breathe freely, without having anything or anyone bounce back to hurt me. Rather funny, considering I was in the land of the grizzly. I still carry not only the memory of feeling expansive and free, but the effect of that experience, which was the **relaxation of unnecessarily held barriers**. In short, I do not expect people to hurt me like I used to.

Every single habit had to be changed. I had to saw wood, carry water from the river, cook on a wood stove, deal with mice having parties on my floor every night (it was their cabin, after all), and adapt to spending long hours in a small dark cabin whose tiny windows were opaque with plastic. I went there close to Equinox, when there was twelve hours of nighttime. By the time I left, there was no night. On cloudy days, I could neither see the sun rise or set, nor the moon, so I could orient none of my activities based on time. I only had a tiny hand mirror, useful for emergencies like getting something in your eye, but I didn't look at myself the whole time. **I could only act from the inside out.**

Rethinking the why, how and when of every task is a way of recreating yourself. In the bush, cultural norms don't apply. Without others to consider, **you will cultivate independent thinking.** Back in regular life, you will feel the freedom to be weird, with the corollary strength to stand in your own truth.

I've since learned that whatever tangent your weirdness takes you on is where you will find your talents in serving others. Later on, doing the foundation year of jungle isolation in Peru, I felt free to vocalize gibberish and sing off key. This led to Anna and Michael singing, and then talking, through me in their language and then in mine. It's common, in that jungle tradition, that people **come out of isolation being experts** in unique forms of massage, art, music and other healing work **with no formal training**.

Without entertainment, there's no fooling yourself. Who are you when there's nothing to do, and no one else around? I saw myself as a spiritual person. I know Buddhists who meditate 12 hours per day and enjoy it. I wasn't even close to that 'ideal.' The prayers I developed to do every day should have taken an hour; I stretched them into four, if I could, just to kill the time. Where was my devotion, worship, delight in nature? I had some unbelievably great moments with the birds, moose, mink, mice, otter and caribou but they only lasted a few minutes each time. I've heard it said that what you do every day is your religion. It became painfully clear that my religion was chewing, or trying not to chew. This **grounding**

into the reality of who I was -- not very impressive, I judged--was useful.

One day in June I found myself pulling weeds out of the rose bushes with sudden anger. Why? There was no one there to be angry at. **Nature offers a perfect mirror**. Only I generated that anger, and only I could dissect and dissolve it. **Know thyself**, and free your loved ones from you projecting your difficult feelings onto their actions. For the record, I did try to blame the weeds but it didn't work.

At the same time, I needed relationships. I would like to say I swam on the backs of caribou, like one of my Tlingit friends later told me he did with his brothers as a kid, but no. I started talking to my rabbit-fur cap, which merited friendship because it had once been attached to a live body (although at a cost of $12 I wasn't sure the fur was real).

"Hat," I would say, taking it off the hook. "Let's go out-side."

I befriended Fire as well, because it felt alive. To this day I get a rush of joyful familiarity when I see a wood fire. Believe me, spend enough time alone and you will be gifted with **a profound appreciation for the gift of having other people to interact with**. Stop sliding into disrespect and taking other people for granted, please!

Sometimes when I lay in bed the whole frame would vibrate to the degree that I thought an earthquake was happening. It took quite a while for me to puzzle out that the source was a jet flying 30,000 feet overhead. In the absence of the bombardment of the artificial vibrations devastating our 'civilized' life, the effect of this single one was shocking. My heart cried for the animals and plants helplessly subjected to this bombardment almost everywhere in the world.

Each man-made vibration buzzes at a single frequency, while natural ones vary in a harmonic symphony. Only in the purity of nature could I merge truly with the natural rhythms of licking flames, rushing river water, currents of pure air and land creatures untainted by mankind. The soothing aspect of this was subtle, and took time to be felt, but was extraordinarily healing. **Being so long in nature changed the imprint of my energetic body.** A couple of times, for example, a bird landed on my head. I must have exuded a similar vibration to a tree. As a shamanic practitioner, I know the value of calling forth those vibrations to serve others -- something I could not do with veracity until I had merged with them purely.

Pare life down to the essentials, in order to find out what's really important to you. In this cabin, my priorities changed drastically. The simple gifts of heat, water, food and shelter became a source of almost worship. How often do we say, "Thank you?" for the comforts that give us such freedom? Items that cost pennies in a grocery store, like nails and string, soared into the 'extremely valuable' category and I strained to re-use them.

My survival depended on my health. Not only were proper eating and exercise habits a necessity, but spontaneous bursts of gratitude filled my heart whenever I did things like lighting a fire with wood I had worked to get. Work itself --

the gift of being able to use the body, mind, and intuition to create a desired result -- is a privilege.

These simple sources of happiness, even pleasure, displaced the entertainments that I didn't bring with me. The animal sightings and the spectacular scenery were a calm source of joy. Yet ... none of these were enough. For example, when I was lighting a fire my eye started catching on the news headlines in the six-months-old newspapers I had brought with me for fire-starter. Imagine my embarrassment when I found myself avidly reading Dear Abby!

The enforced dullness did not do what I intended it to. I remember one two-week period in particular. The melting snow was too soft for snowshoes and too deep for walking with boots. I spent most of that time lying in bed struggling with my chewing addiction.

Yuck. That's what failure feels like.

You did fail. You failed to understand the lesson you learned so well.

Huh?

Exactly. Ho-hum. Life without people is ... life itself is ... simply dull. You bottomed out. The absence of all entertainment revealed that life without Love is pointless. This is our problem. Your culture has busy-ness. It is false. Nothing is good without God. We are allowed only to lift anyone who asks. All other people are busy. Where do we see them in the future world? We don't. They are going to die unhappy because they have left us, Love, behind. Very clearly, you found out that Love is the only thing worth living for. Whether you go to a cabin or develop this value judgement earlier in your spiritual career, you will discover it sooner or later.

I wish I had discovered it sooner. I felt quite desperate. Why live? That was my constant question. Not that I was depressed. Even with my chewing, I never lost hope. I always wondered why that was.

Because we were with you. Even though we weren't ... ahem ... on speaking terms, you had us in mind. That's why you had that instruction to go to the cabin. You needed to empty so that we could fill you with Love.

But I didn't leave there feeling good. I didn't get the result I wanted: the bursting forth of spontaneous Love. So often, I had heard, "Love is who you are." I didn't find it.

Yes. That inner drive for what you call Love is natural. We call it God. What you yearn for is God. Yet most people substitute other things. What did you find out by eliminating everything?

That life is empty.

Right. It is.

You mean we are all scrabbling around searching for emptiness?

Yes. Without God, you are not alive. There is no substitute.

Fire, and a rabbit fur hat, did not do it.

Neither did the vague idea you had that your intuition would develop your spirituality. It is different. Many people think that listening to their inner voice is 'it.' It isn't. Guidance does come through an inner voice. But God is a direct, personal feeling of goodness. It is us, an Alive presence, ready to simply nurture you into your true nature.

Then why do we seek relationship with other people?

Because God is in each of you. The deeper the conversation, the better, right? In those moments, you are talking to God. Even more satisfying is having us as your new best friend, available from the inside out.

"Don't we have to clear out our crap before we can let you in?" you ask. "That's what it sounds like Anna Michael Krista did, or at least went to extremes to do."

That's the message I am here to give you. You don't. I went to these extremes unnecessarily. Well, not totally because I can use them to teach you that you don't need to grind it out the way I did. In a few short months, they have nurtured my basic goodness, and brought me *Alive,* way more than what I laboriously achieved in 19 years.

"Are solo retreats still necessary then?"

Yes. In some form, personal communion with us is absolutely, and joyfully, required. Yet, as you will read in the next sections, it can come through other means.

Chapter 13.5

Service Retreats

"Who are they, deep inside?" he was always asking. "How can I reach them? What can I say to lift them today? To impact them, so that they wake up to the bliss of life that most of them are missing?"

What spiritual path does not include some form of karma yoga? Giving to the poor? Spreading compassion?

We are here to tell you that it's true. These forms of loving yourself are highly approved.

"What do you mean, loving yourself?" you ask.

Seeing, feeling, savouring and believing in your ability to see, feel, savour and believe in another. In a nutshell, that's it.

"Simple delight. That's what I feel when helping others."

Learning to love life in all its variants is what serving others does. Without even focusing on them, it dissolves your own issues. In the same way that the solo retreat will lift you into an appreciation of others, a serving retreat will lead you into appreciating yourself. You will see beauty in every aspect of our creation. Plus, you will deeply ground into your foundation of Self.

"I feel like it increases my selfishness. To be truthful, I serve others because it makes me feel good."

Self-centered is what we are referring to. Serving others will build your sense of who you are. God in a body. That feeling of goodness is us. The more you serve others, the easier you will become embodied.

"Because I am a good person for doing so? Like a reward? Yuck."

I agree. When I was volunteering at Iona Abbey, the cradle of Christianity in Scotland dating from 563 AD, I heard a minister there preach that whoever donated to the book store drive would be absolved from sin for an entire year. Talk about crap!

"What kind of work were you doing there?"

I was folding bedsheets. Doing laundry. Now that part, I enjoyed. It gave me a chance to ponder. Contemplate. Feel my feelings.

"Did you serve others while you were there?"

In a non-structured way. I did make friends, and we helped each other. For example, there was a lesbian minister from Texas there volunteering at the same time. She helped me to separate the teachings of Jesus from the bogus Christianity I was witnessing. Another woman, in a special moment, hugged me to her chest while I cried and wouldn't let me go, the way a mother is supposed to. I touched a young woman who was desperately needing a friend, and she did the same for somebody else.

These were the reasons I loved volunteering at different spiritual centers while I was a nomad. It's enriching to be with others who are on their path. The tradition we were in wasn't important to me. A simple desire to be a better person was what bound us together. That is where we could meet, share, laugh and support each other.

To me, the ideal is that we shift to a culture of helping, where it's only natural to be on the lookout for opportunities to be helpful, because when the god within me meets the god within you, I feel good.

"Does my god meeting your god make it easier to be embodied?" you ask.

Absolutely. God always wants more god. Essentially, you are practicing being god.

"I decided to volunteer on a rotary drive to knock on doors, notifying people of an upcoming event. It felt good, saying hello and seeing how other people lived. But most of the time I was thinking about getting home and having a cup of tea."

It felt empty?

"A little. I suppose it helped."

I'm sure it helped a lot. You just didn't feel good. Why?

"I feel rather helpless. Physical suffering I can't even touch. In that drive, I wanted to get to know people, but the exchanges we had were banal. Pleasant, but a little forced. I didn't feel like I reached anyone. How can I help them if I don't know them?"

You just haven't been trained to ask. It's this simple. You touch someone on the shoulder, look in their eyes, introduce yourself, and say, "I care. Can I help?"

"To a stranger?"

Yes. Allow me to ignite you with an example.

When Michael, the man I declared was the love of my life, died at the age of 38, his sister was shocked at how letters and cards of sympathy poured in from all over the world. He was a simple street vendor who sold his black and white photographs as a guise in order to get by. His true purpose, he informed me, was to help others feel their sensitivities and develop their feminine sides -- both men and women -- which he had experienced as vacant in our society.

This precision of purpose affected all his actions. He took photos that people couldn't help but respond to emotionally, and used the selling of them as an excuse to teach people the lessons of life that he had painstakingly learned. Simplicity was his watchword, and he offered as much information, freely, as a person would absorb. He fully loved every aspect of his life, even when the way the world worked depressed him.

"I can teach you how to take photographs like these in four minutes," he stated as an opening, the first time I met him. He proceeded to do so, eventually in great depth, selflessly giving me hours upon hours of detailed instruction. We poured over each photo of mine that I felt was good enough to show him, illuminating its implications in the fields of psychology, sociology, spirituality and anthropology.

I liked to think he did this because he liked me. Actually, he liked teaching. It made him feel like the struggles he had gone through were worthwhile. In that way, it wasn't as selfless as it seemed. At the same time, there's no way he would have taken a dime for all his time. That would have cheapened it, in his mind.

He had a gift of the gab, a charismatic presence. This helped enormously to impress people, along with his flair for style in dressing. He was a small man, a high school drop-out, had no presence in the official world, and struggled for enough money to eat and pay his rent. He liked that though, because it made each day an adventure. He capitalized on his charisma to the advantage of others. Anybody who came his way was a target.

"Who are they, deep inside?" he was always asking. "How can I reach them? What can I say to lift them today? To impact them, so that they wake up to the bliss of life that most of them are missing?" That is what drove him, not just as he was selling his images, but as he moved through the world. Why did this work for him? One big reason. He felt himself to be good enough to help others.

The spontaneity of life was within him. Creativity permeated his every action. He had fun, and that was contagious. He had tears in his eyes, one day, telling me about three young men whom he had been talking to for quite a while. When it came time to say goodbye, each of the three eagerly reached out to shake his hand in the same moment. He described it as a priceless payment for his time.

His life was the epitome, in my experience at the time, of how to help others.

I tried to do it his way. It didn't work.

Many an hour I sat in coffee shops, putting out feelers to the people around me, trying to find openings to make suggestions. Few arose. Why? Because I do not have the personality that he did. I am shy. Forcing what didn't come naturally didn't work.

"Okay, so how do I go about it?" you wonder.

Your gifts are unique. Exploration is required. Trying equals learning. Actually, it doesn't matter what you do, or how successful you are. It doesn't matter whether your motive is selfish or altruistic. Just do it. You will evolve into something bigger than you, into the grand oneness. With your invitation, Anna and Michael will help you, because that is who they are.

When I was suffering the most, in Peru, I was also having nightly experiences of awe with God.

"Please, may others feel this good," I would say. "Somehow, make me useful." Yet every day I did nothing to help others. I felt bad about it at the time. Look what happened. Now I am finally feeling useful, in a way that is perfectly suited to me.

For eight months I volunteered as kitchen manager at Salt Spring Yoga Center, a place created by several followers of Baba Hari Dass, a saint who has kept silence since 1952. One morning the lead administrator, a woman named Anuradha, passed through the kitchen as I was pulling some burnt cookies out of the oven.

"Too bad," she said mildly, picking one up and taking a bite out of a good part, and continuing on her way.

"She certainly didn't used to be like that," said one other administrator, when I mentioned this incident with admiration. "She's learned a lot of wisdom in how to manage people," she said. "At one time, she would have been really angry at the waste and ineptitude."

This small example of Anuradha's grace testifies that her twenty-plus years of working selflessly, tirelessly and without getting paid to help people who came there for various programs did her the greatest good. As a side effect, the openings she created by not judging others was an invitation for the volunteer staff to go to her with their problems. This was not her job; it just happened. She was well loved.

In the same way, whatever you do to help others will develop your abilities, in some fashion, on all levels. Karma yoga, as a spiritual path, is tried and true.

"Sure, I get it. I do help, whenever I can. I like to make a difference. But I can't devote myself to it the way these people have. I need to make a living, and spending time with my family is a priority."

Do you consider yourself to be part of the Family of Man? Aren't we in a planetary crisis? Your help is needed more than ever before. Say, 'Yes' to Anna and Michael, and they will help you help others exponentially, in a way that doesn't just work with your other commitments, but aids them. For example, it's important to me to live near my mom, who is in a care home. Anna and Michael have taken advantage of my visits there to teach me, in little ways, how to serve others.

"What if they want you to live somewhere else in the future, and your mom can't live with you?"

I made caring for my mom the one non-negotiable part of our covenant. If it was absolutely imperative that I leave this area, they would ensure that she was cared for just as lovingly. They would do their best to make sure it didn't last too long.

"I see a chicken and egg problem here. I need to be embodied to help effectively, but in order to facilitate embodiment I need to dedicate time and money that I don't have because I am not yet skilled enough."

The highest calling, the most difficult path with the highest reward, is to say, 'Yes' and trust that it will all work out, without you controlling anything. It's a tall order. I can tell you though; it will be better than anything you can do alone, and better than anything you have ever dreamed.

"But you were alone, without any dependents, and with a financial security blanket. You had the freedom to pursue your dream. I don't. You were desperately ill, but I'm not. Besides, I've seen other fanatics try to live without money. I don't know how your Anuradha did it, but it just doesn't work. Not in this society."

I understand the arguments, believe me. I have very little income, have lived below the poverty line for almost 20 years, and now Anna and Michael are asking me to spend money freely, while working for donations only. In return, they guarantee me goodness and love. In my weak moments, I retort, "Goodness can come in the form of lessons, and that could mean I'm learning how to love while I am living on the street!"

Yet in my strong moments, I have no doubt. I will spend every penny I have, if need be. Deposit myself on the doorstep of another spiritual center, and whine until they take me in, if I have to. The Love that Anna and Michael lift me with is worth it. Plus, they do promise they will support me financially, because it is in their best interest to have me available to them.

"What about me? Are they going to support me too?"

That's a question you will have to answer for yourself. It depends how far you choose to go.

"Are you suggesting I risk everything to serve others?"

Jesus said to go as far as losing your physical life, in order to serve others. We're not going that far. Yet in a sense, all my suggestions for retreats are about risking your life, or what you think/feel you need in order to survive. The closer you are to death, the more you realize you have nothing to lose and everything to gain by living free. Be cautious, think it through, but figure out a way to do whatever it takes. Keep going until you find what that is for you. Therein lies the adventure.

Chapter 13.6

Adventure Retreats

This is the classic story of the hero's journey. You go into the unknown, face dangers, go down false paths, build friendships, and come out the other side a better person.

In my twenties, my life was stultifyingly predictable. I was married before I finished university, and started working for IBM as soon as I finished. I had back problems and neck pain that gave me headaches that lasted two or three days twice a week. We bought a house, we visited my in-laws and my family, he fished and I took up golf. We chatted with our elderly neighbours sometimes. Other people lead lives like this and enjoy them, but I didn't, because my feeling frequency was a monotone. That is, I went through the motions but very little reached the inside me.

My feelings were still there, but unconscious. Without appropriate expression, they came out sideways and I had an affair. Needless to say, my marriage ended.

The man Michael woke me up to the tragedy that not only could I not articulate my feelings, I barely felt them. I was numb. No wonder I felt as stiff as the tin man from *The Wizard of Oz*. My heart and I weren't connected.

My nomadic quest, in fact my entire spiritual quest, was one of reaching my feelings.

It started in Cape Breton. I didn't sit all those hours in front of a mirror seeking a calm and peaceful mindfulness. Here's an excerpt from my journal at that time, after I had been sitting for at least two months.

On the last night I saw Michael, he asked me, "What are you going to do in Cape Breton?"

I replied, "I'll get up there and say, "What the heck have I done?" Then I'll say, "What the heck am I doing?" Then I'll say, "What the heck am I going to do?"

But those questions have never plagued me. Since I've come here, every second has felt totally right. I can be sitting on that straight-backed chair for hours, then be doubled over with my elbow in my guts looking at my contorted face in the mirror, conscious of the cat perking up at my animal-like sounds of pain, (my version of crying), and feel this is the most wondrous thing I have ever experienced.

Yesterday I was writhing on the floor trying to cry. Crying because I couldn't cry. Beating the floor with my feet and fists trying to beat away that damned mind of mine, cursing those layers of self-control I painstakingly cultivated over the years. The tears squeezed out one by one, more out of frustration than primal pain. Why? Why couldn't I cry? Why couldn't I let it out in uncontrolled sobs, retching in every fiber of my being?

Last night I dreamed why.

Bones from a skeleton arose from an opening in the earth. They assembled into a human form and stood up beside me, saying, "I'm crazy about you."

Hurrah! I am resurrected!

Later, he hissed at me, "You have to die first."

Later again, I was stopped from doing something I wanted to do. I asked the Being why.

He said, "You still don't know, do you? The hurt is going to come closer than you."

So that is my answer. The resurrection has begun, but the real pain is beneath me, buried so completely it does not exist at all in my conscious self. That conscious self, my ego self, has to die first. If that being is my real Self, then my pain lies between it and me.

I have to kill me now.

All morning, the question has been plaguing me. How do I die? It would be easier to carve my own breast, or to swallow a chemical death, than to let go the bulldog grip of this oh-so-rational mind.

Knowing that I couldn't kill myself, that it had to be done *to* me, I pleaded to the moon, night upon night.

"Break me down, please. Break me through to my true feelings. Do whatever it takes. I know it'll be hard, but in the end, I'll be a better person. I know I'll be okay. Mother Nature will take care of me."

That plea was like a vow in which I gave permission to God to kill me.

I started taking risks. I walked alone in the moonlight, in nature and in cities. I backpacked across Britain, hitch-hiking at times. I hiked parts of the Appalachian Trail, and dove into classes at the Tom Brown school, even sojourning in a tent for a winter in the Pine Barrens of New Jersey. I pulled into Whitehorse on December 17th, just to test how I would react to not knowing anyone at Christmas time. I went on long-distance canoe trips with complete strangers, and even took trips alone. I tested my mettle against the most stringent spiritual practices I could find: long hours of meditation, solo retreats, fasting, vision quests, living with others in community.

Adventure is fantastic. It prunes unnecessary habits quickly. It builds character: courage, thoughtful consideration, fortitude, determination and persistence. It tests your resourcefulness, and makes you think creatively. Going beyond your comfort zone helps develop a range of skills and an adaptability so that you can be useful wherever you go.

By making mistakes and learning from them, you start to trust yourself, to make good decisions and to consider others. Striking out with others toward a common goal makes you realize how much you need them, especially their differences. Surviving difficult situations makes you feel proud, capable, and like you are a good human being, ready and able to tackle the next unknown thing. It has to be fun, but a good adventure plumbs the depths of all your emotions: excitement, fear, joy, sadness, love, anger and even hatred. It's exercising the full feeling spectrum that gives the satisfaction of time well spent.

Over time, the adventurous life pried me open and I started to respond more in the moment, in an authentic way, to my environment rather than to half-forgotten and compounded memories of childhood situations. Yet the more the external worked toward the internal, the less satisfying the external became. The form of the adventure would change, but the content, once fully lived, did not need to be lived again.

This is the classic story of the hero's journey. You venture alone into the unknown, face dangers, go down false paths, build friendships, and come out the other side a better person. Then you bring your better self home, content to share it until the next adventure beckons.

External adventure never did kill me in the way I anticipated. But when I asked the question, "What do I need to do before I die," I eventually got the answer 'nothing.' My bucket list was empty.

The ultimate adventure is internal. All the time Anna Michael Krista was nomadic, she was searching for us. She used the external adventure as a guise for that. That guise can be anything. The family adventure. The solo adventure. The simple life adventure. The business adventure. Life itself is an adventure. Your development requires you to carve out specific events you call adventure. These triggers help you to feel alive. But the true Alive comes from us.

I never would have known this if I hadn't taken the internal journey with ayahuasca. But once I discovered God in those sacred ceremonies, I had no more need for outer adventure. In fact, I always laugh at how boring my adventures in Peru seem to other people. I've only ever stayed at one healing center. I haven't been to Cuzco, haven't traversed Machu Picchu, and I haven't tripped down the Amazon. Once I get to Peru, I only want to go to God.

What ayahuasca has shown me is that the adventure is endless. There is a continuum, starting from the inside of each of us, rippling into the vast unknown and normally unseen universe of places, beings and creatures. It's as infinitely wide as it is long, and no one being could ever experience it all. Better than *Star Trek*, where no one has gone before, it's also a co-creation. It opens a person to an intelligence that has an obvious purpose for the greater good, which includes you. The felt, seen, and understood experience of unbelievable genius leaves people awestruck, and loving life as never before.

Yet it wasn't everything. Much as it healed me, thrilled me and made me bow down in worship, my daily life was still a struggle. I still hadn't gotten down to the essence of my neurosis: my feelings and experiences of love in the journeys were estranged from my daily life. I was not yet *Alive*.

As you read in my story of horrific growing pains, joining with Michael and Anna simply upped the ante of adventure to twenty-four hours a day. Yes, I was feeling my feelings: wonky, perverted, leftover remnants from a million disappointing moments in my youth. Or perhaps from before I was born.

Yet believe it or not, even after those inner and all my outer adventures, I was still to experience the biggest adventure of all. And it happened at home, in my tame apartment, lying substance-free on my couch.

Once I gave Anna and Michael full, sincere permission to help me become a better person, they zeroed in on my feelings with a scalpel. The trappings of outer adventure, and the spectacular phenomena of inner journeys, were cast aside in favour of getting down to business: eradicating those remnants of fear, anger and sadness. Even hatred. In my case, mostly, fear.

Chapter 13.7

The Feeling Adventure

In spite of my crap, in spite of my mistakes, in spite of the things I knew I could have done better, I was and am still the same good person. Lovable. Huggable. Smileable. Laughable, too.

Tell me about your day. What event triggered your feelings, made you feel the deepest?

"Oh, gosh. There was so much. My sister called and ... I was late for xxx and regretted missing so-and-so ... Ah, I saw this little girl running as though she loved life."

Did you stop to cherish that love in yourself?

"Well, the thought passed through. But then I had to get to my next appointment."

This 'too-busy' scenario is all too common, and it's not going anywhere soon. Much as this culture is on the fulcrum of a huge change for the better, for the foreseeable future we are going to stay busy.

Catching a few minutes here and there, perhaps in a yoga class or by taking a walk, to catch up with yourself -- that is, to literally re-align your emotional, intellectual, physical and spiritual bodies -- is not enough. Periodic maintenance is required. And that's just to stay on top of daily life.

Deeper work is required to stop those persnickety feelings buried via childhood trauma from tripping you up, ruling your life and killing your enjoyment of others.

You are, I am and we all are foundationally good people. What happened?

"I always have good intentions," you say.

So does everyone. What is the problem? We execute ineffectively. We are never taught the simple basics of feeling, communicating those feelings, and sharing difficult feelings.

Anna and Michael have been teaching me, and others, how to do this. I am in awe. It's so simple. At the root of every single difficult and great feeling can be found one statement: I care.

You feel scared? It's because you care about life and want to protect it. You hate someone or something? It's because you care about making life better. You feel sad, disappointed or stuck in despair? It's because you care about life and wish it could be different.

What do you do with this caring? You lie, cheat, steal, manipulate, cajole, avoid, impress and use any number of other strategies to avoid saying this one thing: I care. Why?

Because before, when you've expressed your sensitivities, you've been hurt.

Where are your hurt feelings kept? You speak them and they flow. When you don't speak them, they stick, typically in your body, memories and thoughts. Sticky thoughts re-route thinking patterns, skewing them to your advantage ... you think. At first, they are linked with the memories. But time goes on, the memories fade and the perverted thought patterns rule your decision-making. Unexpressed and unacknowledged, they start ruling your body. Unconsciously, a hundred or a thousand times a day, you cringe in fear, seize with hatred, clutch with sadness, and inflame with anger.

This should be balanced by good feelings, right?

Wrong. Too much of the time, you feel guilty when you feel good.

"Oh, that's just ego," you slap yourself. "Sure, I did something good, but not as good as someone else could have." Then, rather than celebrating when someone else does something good, you secretly gloat, "I could have done a better job than they did."

Anna and Michael have helped others, through me, recognize their unfelt feelings and get them flowing again. Why? Because these complexes of feelings stop us from helping others. Our myopic self-concern distracts us and barricades us to the point where we don't even see what others are going through.

More than that. We don't enjoy life. We don't feel good, 99% of the time. When is the last time you laughed helplessly? When is the last time you felt just plain good, for no reason? When is the last time you felt like dancing as you walked down the street? Did you do it?

These steady good feelings come from knowing that you are loved, all the way through.

"But I was, as a child. Although I am lucky. Most of my friends weren't."

You weren't either. No matter how good it was, what is available is new. True Mother's Love. Anna has come forth to feel us into her natural existence. I can tell you that it's a Love that we've almost never known before, because I've experienced it. This entire book is a plea, both to you and to Her, that you feel Her, and as a result feel anchored in your own good, regardless of what is going on in your outer existence. Yet only the experience of Her will do that.

She did this for me via a series of feeling adventures, which I called 'The Fires of Purification.' Day after day, for weeks, we ended up lying on the couch. I had to be lying down because She would take over my body, my feelings and my voice to make me experience, all the way through, what She was teaching me. We used situations as they arose in daily life, plus, as I came to realize, She created situations in my daily life that were perfectly designed to trigger me into my essential fears.

As I was going through this process, there is no way I could have held a job. Choosing to work with Anna and Michael means you must be open, at any moment, for them to stop you, and to make you notice something, feel something or try something. Better than the best of gurus you have heard of, they act in the moment, using any resource currently available optimally. What they do depends not only on your conscious decisions, words and actions, but on your unacknowledged feelings and choices you've made so habitually you don't even know you did it.

That's why you must carve out a special time to do this work. It's imperative that you declare a start time and a stop time; they will work within that framework and, by the way, care for your family responsibilities while you are in it. They want this to happen as much or more than you do, and will meet you more than halfway to make it happen lovingly.

As best as I could, using a digital recorder and a notebook and blogging as soon as I could, I documented these sessions. The following excerpt will give you a flavor for how Anna and Michael rooted out my solidly entrenched fear of failure, with my retrospective comments in brackets. At the time, I didn't yet have the names Anna or Michael, and referred to them as "my Friend."

Can I love while I am doing my mom's taxes?

My bliss bubble from the day before had faded. I was on task, and had told my Friend that I needed a few hours to fulfil my commitment (to myself) that I would do this today.

While I was executing efficiently, my Friend occasionally spoke up.

What Love is, is what you are.

Smile. I would pause, let the reality that I am Love permeate through my illusion that I was still who I used to be, and then get back to work.

What you love is what you are.

Smile.

Wait a minute. If I am doing my taxes, and don't feel loving while I am doing them, then I am displacing Love with devotion to being efficient. What was I loving right now? Who was my God now?

(Noticed how doubt has kicked in, as they intended.)

Choose Love and it will choose you.

Okay, that means I just have to keep choosing Love while I am doing the taxes. Keep "I am Love" as the running commentary of my inner dialogue.

Could you love more?

(Here is where they dug into my incessant questing for how to be a better person.)

"That's enough. I need to get back on task. We can have a lesson when I'm done."

I could love you ...

That phrase rankled. It was ridiculous, because I knew my Friend loved me, so why put the conditional slant on it? Punishing my Friend in my mind, I finished my task, took the dog for a walk, and lay down on the couch.

"Okay, now we can have the lesson."

I could love you, if you love me.

"Yes, I could have loved you more. But I had to get things done. I thought we had been through this?"

What could you do, if you loved more?

"I can generate more Love with my mind. But after yesterday, with Love being ALL, that feels fake."

I could love you, if you love me.

"I do love you, just not in this moment. What's with all these riddles anyway?"

If you loved me more, you would love yourself more.

"You want to get me upset? All right. In this moment, I choose not to Love you. There, that's the truth."

I am rapidly being driven into a pout.

"Do you really think I am up for all this?"

Could you be more perfect?

I relaxed. I *am* perfect for the job.

(Then my doubts re-entrench themselves.)

Uh-oh. Perhaps my Friend meant that I *could* be more perfect! What a perfect dig into my feelings of imperfection!

Could you love me for the first time?

By this time the bliss bubble was nowhere to be found.

"No," I said petulantly. "I am a little child when it comes to knowing how to love. A little child who was never loved right. But I've been through all this. Blaming Mom and Dad, rooting out my issues ..."

Put Love First, my Friend interrupted my rant.

(This was an instruction that derived out of my purification prayers to the Supreme God, The First Source and Universal Center. In this moment, I did not want to do this for the precise reason that they were telling me to. I don't like being told what to do.)

I stuck out my tongue, allowing myself to get right into it.

(I had enough experience to know that whatever they were doing, however uncomfortable it might be, it would be worthwhile.)

"F-off. Go away. F-you for the first time!" I squirmed. I don't like that word. I can't even write it out in full. But I did say it.

I was in old, old feelings of being ugly, but still enough of a 'witness' to be writing down the conversation in my notebook.

Could you love me?

"No. Obviously not. Why am I even bothering to write this down? It's useless anyway. No one will read it. Forget it."

Of course I couldn't forget it. Turning the irritating phrase back onto my Friend, I asked pointedly, "Could you love me?"

A giggle erupted.

"Could you? Even if I'm not perfect?"

(I lashed out in sarcastic retaliation.)

I knew what my Friend was getting at. I can't love others because I judge them. They are not perfect enough for me. But really, I am not perfect enough for myself. It's all just straightforward psychological neurosis. So what? It's not news to me.

You will be where we are.

Was this encouragement? I chose to stay in my mope.

"Sure, hold that out as a carrot. When? In 50,000 lifetimes?"

The riddles were doing their job as connections clicked about how my see-sawing between inferiority and superiority has kept people from loving me. Kept me from loving people. Tears streamed, my heart heaved and my gut wrenched. It's a long time since I've gotten down to those ugly feelings and stayed there. For over a decade, I've used physical pain as a substitute for feeling. Since I stopped that last summer, (miraculously, and thanks only to my Friend and God), I've been surprised that more emotion hasn't overtaken me.

(Notice how I think the lesson is about analyzing my past.)

Put the first lesson first.

Huh?

The first lesson in the Way of Love is Honesty.

My mind jumped ahead. My Friend had referred lately to the fourth, the fifth, and been counting up to seven. I didn't catch the meaning, but I could instantly see a structure of seven lessons on how to Love, laid out nicely in an e-book or taught in a class.

(Grasping onto the idea that I was being taught something I could hold onto, I felt a bit better.)

Humbled at the reams of examples of how I had pushed people away, I peeped, "I'm getting better, though, aren't I?"

I was thinking of a morning conversation in which I had told a new friend about the healing work that I do. I thought I had introduced the idea, without being pushy about it, rather well. But should I have been more honest?

"Should I have told her directly that I thought it would benefit her?"

(See how I assumed I had done something wrong? Noticing this reaction, they drove my insecurities deeper.)

You should have asked her to love you.

Ouch! Was I that self-serving, that I wanted her to come to a healing session so she could experience how good I am at it, so that then she would like/love me more? I spun into a pit of guilt and shame.

(Exactly where they wanted me to go: feeling like a failure.)

I didn't bounce out of it after the crying wore out. I took the dog for a walk but squelched out hurt feelings with every step. Knowing that it was all useful didn't pull me out of my pain.

Remembering my dream the next morning didn't help either. A friend had wanted to buy a house that looked okay on the outside but was beat up, crooked and stained on the inside. With a huge bright yellow kitchen! Just like me -- twisted and warped inside and focusing far too much on food.

(They used this dream to reinforce my feelings of not being good enough.)

I like to ponder my dreams, and my latest lessons, without moving my body one iota after I wake up. It anchors them. It was in that rumination about how awful I was that illumination burst forth.

"It was all about me beating myself up, wasn't it?" I asked my Friend.

He sighed a heaving *Yes.*

"I could love you if ..." was not a condition put forth by my Friend. It was simply a reflection of my own thoughts. My root insecurity. I know I am an honest person. But the comment about honesty fired my belief that I am not honest enough. To be more accurate, *I am not enough.* I don't love myself as I am.

To experience the bubble of bliss, the Love of God, is indescribable. To know with certainty that I am not who I think I am, that rather I am Love, is an unbelievable blessing. But when I fall back into identifying with my habits and patterns as being who I am, it is vital that I love and fully accept that as well.

For living is being with what is, said my Friend this morning. *Loving is being who you are now. I love you now. Whoever you are.*

I am enough. I am good enough. I will never be a better person, because I was born a good person, I am still that good person, and I will always be just that good of a person. This theme dominated these weeks of purification until I not only believed it, but felt this goodness all the way through every ounce of my being.

In spite of my crap, in spite of my mistakes, in spite of the things I knew I could have done better, I was and am still the same good person. Lovable. Huggable. Smileable. Laughable, too.

I still get scared. I still feel small. I still get flashes of inferiority/superiority. I am subject to all the human flaws you can imagine. Yet, I feel good about myself. All the other feelings ripple through my daily life the way they are supposed to. When I take myself too seriously, don't get it, or start sinking into that "I'm not good enough," feeling, they make something ridiculous out of it so that I can't help but laugh. They love me. Unstoppably, unconditionally, and unerringly.

"I appreciate you sharing your experience," you say. "Yet frankly, it sounds like just another session. Psychology, dream analysis, bodywork, past life regression -- they all amount to the same result. Digging into and releasing childhood trauma."

What those sessions are typically missing is Divine Love. When you dig into and unravel a significant complex, it leaves a hole behind. Have you ever had the experience of feeling released, and having the same feelings crop up in a new situation? Love is the answer. It fills the gaps. I have viscerally experienced an old thought pattern being bypassed by Michael and Anna so that I don't detour down that route. But you cannot love yourself enough. Michael and Anna directly caring for you, with all the attention you never received as a child, is imperative. You need to feel it 24/7, forever, for you to not fall back into those gaps.

They sustain me. If I wasn't with them, my good feelings would fluctuate again. I would be back to the uncertain emptiness that I felt before. I know this for a fact, because they have given me the experience of taking those feelings away, just so that I could tell you this. It's not pleasant. It's not fun. And, it's not necessary. I freely admit I need Anna and Michael.

You might wonder how I can write the outrageous things I am writing in this book. How could I have the audacity to state that I am joined with Christ? It is so much a part of my daily truth that I am willing to risk everything -- my reputation, my livelihood, my friends, and my family -- to shout this out to you. Whoever is listening is meant to hear these words. I feel that good. You can too.

You have read about people with near-death experiences, and how they saw and felt Love like never before. That is what is newly available on Earth. The complete absolution of all our mistakes, while still in a body.

Feelings. This segment of this book on feelings is critical. Applying these suggestions to make time for us is necessary. Frankly, we feel along with you. When your feelings are stuck, as so many people suffering from depression are, we are stuck also. We can't reach you. We have taken steps to alleviate this, to ensure stuck feelings loosen more easily than they used to. You may have experienced already a lightening of everyone's life; noticed a few more chuckles, a taking of problems less seriously, coupled with new ways of unsticking glommed-together feelings. This will accelerate.

Right now, medicinal entheogenic plants like ayahuasca are fantastic for releasing stuck feelings. Eventually, we will be able to perform these 'operations' on you without it, as Anna Michael Krista described in her couch session.

It is an operation. These feelings have warped your energetic imprint. When you use our help to re orient them, so that they flow correctly, as designed, through your chakras, your energetic imprint is corrected. We fill the gaps. Love is that. Intelligent, targeted, action that, believe it or not, fixes you.

"You say to take time, but I feel conflicted. I need to devote my attention to my family."

Even better. Read on.

Chapter 13.8

The Family Adventure

Create a bond of interdependence that makes you stick together through thick and thin, just like a blood family is designed to.

Family is the ultimate spiritual adventure.

"Did I hear that right? My family responsibilities take me away from my spiritual path. I would love to carve out a few months for a solo retreat, or to go to Peru, but I just can't."

Hear this. Anna and Michael tell me that ideally, if you approach your everyday family life like the greatest spiritual challenge ever, it will whittle away your extraneous selves and polish your gifts like none of the previous methods can come close to doing. Their vision is of self-assured individuals enjoying each other thoroughly while they team their efforts to synergize new creations. Learning how to work simultaneously as an individual and as a family unit prepares you to work with them for the greater good of the Family of Man.

Moreover, they hold a vested interest in the creation of a new breed of humans. For couples who say, 'Yes' they want to cultivate, co-create and help raise babies who are born joined with them and bask in their full Divine Love from the moment they are first co-visioned by their to-be parents. If you are not partnered now, don't worry. Your intention to parent will be fulfilled. If you are in a homosexual relationship, don't worry. Your intention to parent will be fulfilled. I don't know how, but I know it's true.

From my friends who have children now, though, I hear a vastly different story. Competing claims on their time have them exhausted. The choice between spending time making money to support the kids, and spending time loving the kids, is heart-wrenching. The pressure to 'do' activities leaves everyone scrambling for family time, and the watchword 'quality time' is substituted. Technology seems to be taking over as teacher, and the critical skills of character-building, value prioritization, spiritual awareness, relating to others, ethics and morals are getting lost in the cracks between home and school.

Time out.

Can't or don't want to take time away from the kids? Carve out a spiritual adventure with them as your focus.

"A spiritual adventure?" you protest. "That's the last thing they want to do. My kids need to be entertained."

Wanna bet? Try this. Say to your child, "Who are you? Why are you existing on this planet? What role do you play in this family?" If they have answers, kudos on you. If not, these are the most effective questions you can ask, and they will stimulate your kids far more than technology.

The key is to make it about them. They are the ones least able to speak about what is most important to them. Unless they've been talked with in this fashion since they were very young, they cannot function in this language. Anna and Michael say this is your most important job as a parent. Entertainment is simply a substitute for their cavernous need to feel valued.

Our suggestions? Create a situation where you need each other for entertainment. Cut off the technology. Change the environment so that you are forced to completely re-shuffle the family dynamic. Make games about changing the roles each of you play, to spark mutual appreciation. Change the rules, for a period of time. Better yet, have the kids make the rules for a day. Making every moment new will entertain them, and you will be fully involved.

Make a distraction free vacation. No sightseeing. For this one, forget even the museums and other learning expeditions. Make it physical. Take a canoe trip, or rent a big sailboat, and make sure there's enough time for them to crack through the frustration that the inevitable boredom will bring. Honestly, this kind of adventure will bring your family to a brand new level of love.

"Great advice, but how does that help me embody I AM?"

Imagine your whole family embodied as I AM.

"Wow."

Yes. Ultimately, your whole family could be orchestrated as a unit by Anna and Michael. So far, I have told you about them teaching me from within my body. Imagine them teaching you using the voice of your child. Each member of your family would be individually joined to them; however the lessons would come through any of you, at any time, full of goodness, and exponentially lifting your kids into such radically new awareness and elevated experience that they could be extraordinary leaders of the generations to come.

Let your imagination play with this idea. It hasn't been done yet, on this plane of existence. The potential is infinite.

Meanwhile, creating family adventures helps you personally to prepare for embodiment, because being embodied is kinda like having your entire family inside you, 24/7.

"How so?"

- You are not just in it for yourself. You are working with Anna and Michael for the greatest good of the whole, and your personal desires are secondary (concurrent with your joy being primary, so don't worry about that too much.) In a family, you get practice putting others first. Eventually, you find that what you get back from giving makes you so happy that you are really putting your need for happiness first.

- You cannot hide. Anna and Michael know every nuance of every thought, word and action you take. All your foibles are fully exposed. Sneakiness is still allowed; it's just not secret. Like being in a family, you learn that you are loved, accepted and have a lot to offer even though you are imperfect.
- You never know whose voice carries the most weight. Continually, you are called on to juggle what you know for yourself to be true with what they are telling you. Same with whatever any of your family members comes at you with: it's a dance of discernment that requires ever-present curiosity and a willingness to make mistakes.
- Just like family members, Anna and Michael will come at you with situations that don't feel very good. Treating everything as either good, or a lesson which ultimately ends up being good, is sage advice for any family situation. With Anna and Michael, blaming and resisting only makes you feel worse.
- Family life is an ego equalizer. As often as you are the hero or the sage, you stumble and have to accept that you are no better than someone else. No worse, either, as everyone stumbles as they learn. It's similar with Anna and Michael; after lauding and exploiting

> your gifts with great gusto, they will submerge you in the next lesson such that you come up sputtering with humility.

"That sounds really scary," you say. "I'm not sure I'm ready for that kind of exposure."

You are not used to it. You are used to separating your private and public life. Crazily enough, you often have even more barriers when you are at home with your so-called loved ones.

"You mean, like when the four of us all sitting together texting our friends, and calling that family time?"

Precisely. Here we have a chicken and egg problem. When Anna and Michael are a living presence in your life, they will help each of you dissolve these barriers via the targeted wisdom of Love. Yet, as it stands now, the habitual barriers endemic to our current style of family life impede their entry.

You have to start somewhere, so I suggest you just try. Follow the standard formula we are advising: make the choice, ask for help, give permission and make the time. Something will happen. Even if it doesn't work out the way you planned, remember that your kids are sensitive. They will remember your effort, and feel the love behind it. During your post-event sharings, get the kids to suggest follow-up experiments at home.

Katye Anna's book, *Conscious Construction Of The Soul,* suggests that you and your kids made a contract before you were born to teach each other certain things. Assume this is true, and treat your kids as your teachers, especially in this arena. Their creative capacity is fresh, so tap into it.

"How do you know this stuff? You don't have kids."

No, I don't. But I have spent a lot of time living in close community with others. Many people like me have been working to create psuedo-family experiences, because we crave that intimate connection, and we know there's a better way. All over the world, people are experimenting with various forms of community life.

I lived in one of these in Nova Scotia called EarthSea. One couple, both of them shamanic practitioners, decided, together with their 19-year-old daughter and seven-year-old son, to open up their oceanside house to anyone who wanted to live there. They maintained their privacy upstairs where their bedrooms were. The rest of the small house -- kitchen, bathroom, entry/sitting room and living room -- was completely shared.

The people who came devised their own sleeping arrangement on the land. I stayed in my van, my friends had a teepee, and others built small dwelling shacks. All of us -- about ten at the peak -- took turns gardening, doing chores and making meals. The spiritual teachings and practices of the host couple were freely shared, and many projects for bringing new awareness into the local community were joint adventures.

Weekly meetings, and non-violent communication practices, were used to keep things running smoothly.

This was an extremely generous act on the part of the host couple. They asked for only a fractionated contribution to their electrical bill. Their only requirement for joining was a belief in a higher power, as they felt anyone who showed up on their doorstep added to the adventure.

What a quirky group of people! I only wish we had all been embarking on *The Way Of Alive*™ then. It was a lot of fun anyway, but oh, what extraordinary advances we would have all made, both personally and in terms of group cohesion.

After five months, I decided to move on. I wasn't feeling completely met, and had no idea how to communicate that to the others. They seemed so knowing, so firm in their own ways. I didn't trust that they loved me enough to work with me. In other words, I didn't love myself enough.

These are the people I ran to when I was so scared after being joined with Anna and Michael. Even though I hadn't lived with them for over a decade, the community had disbanded and the individuals involved lived in different locales, being with them felt like being home. On the surface, it looks as though that community failed. But no. The vibes of that effort, and the members' willingness to risk being fully exposed, warts and all, as a means of bettering life on Earth and speeding up their own paths, stand as pillars of achievement in Anna and Michael's world.

It doesn't always work out that beautifully. Yet then the lessons can be even more powerful. I have another story for you, in a sense the complete antithesis to the unstructured, experimental, mistake-prone EarthSea. I spent six months on a work-study program at Pema Chodron's Tibetan monastery in Cape Breton.

The main purpose at the monastery, as I understood it, was to progress toward enlightenment by combining meditation with intense communal living. Within a single building, we all slept, ate, studied and meditated. Four of us slept in one bedroom, (one in a cubbyhole), with only a curtain for privacy. The saving grace of this 'in your face' system was that silence was enforced from 8 p.m. until noon the next day. When meeting another person in the hallway, we were not even obliged to meet their eyes or nod, which allowed me the privacy I felt I needed. When the noon bell rang, the boisterous chatter in the dining room lineup was exuberant because we all so eagerly looked forward to sharing the multitudinous experiences we had enjoyed since 8 p.m. the night before. I was always surprised by how much we all liked each other, living in such close confines. It stemmed from us all being on the same mission -- to be better people -- and the curiosity we had about another's perspective on our shared experience.

Correction. We didn't all like each other. I was one of three cooks, and the kitchen manager hated me. At least it felt that way. For the first week I was there, she cooked with me. We became friends, and she taught me a lot. Then she iced me with zero communication. How can you do this and give someone instruction? She would write me notes. Most of the time she would leave them for me, but sometimes she would deliberately turn her back to me, while talking to someone else, and jut the note at me from behind her back. It was not nice.

I had come from EarthSea, and the Tom Brown school, where non-violent communication was a skill we were all practicing. The Buddhist way was different.

"Just go sit on a cushion," was the recommendation. Any discomfort you were having, presumably, would dissolve on its own. There was a system for bringing concerns about others to an objective third party, and although I went through this process, my manager did not cooperate. She simply kept ignoring me.

My habit of blaming myself for interpersonal dysfunction was relieved after about a month, when another woman shared with me that this manager had done the identical thing to her. After learning that it was not a problem I caused, I gave up on solving it and steadfastedly resorted to sourcing my self-esteem in that job from my own feeling of goodness and from knowing that I was connected to God. The fact that people ate what I cooked helped, but in that environment, where food is almost the sole source of entertainment, pretty much anything tastes good. Plus, since eating what is offered is part of the practice, complaining is not advised.

Before I went in to the monastery, a Buddhist friend had advised that when I wanted to run from the place, which he predicted I would, to stick it out.

"It's only six months of your life," he said. "Whatever happens, use it for all it's worth as a lesson."

Keeping his advice in mind, hundreds of times a day I would tell myself to let those feelings of frustration and hurt go. I don't know if I ever did, but I did get resigned to the situation, and gave up on fixing it.

I didn't realize how deeply that giving up permeated my being until several weeks after I left the monastery. While visiting my brother at the family cottage, he invited me to go water-skiing, something my dad raised us all to do well. Much to my surprise, when I waved him to hit the throttle, and felt the pull of the rope, I let go of the handle, limply sliding off the dock into the water. He swung the boat around, I got back up on the dock, and we tried again, but the same thing happened. I was completely befuddled, until I remembered that for about five seconds, it's critical to brace your legs with all your strength to get up. You have to resist, and I had forgotten how to do that. I had given up ... far too easily!

A few lessons here. Our experience deeply etches its way

into our habitual patterns, such that we don't even know we have them. That's why it's essential to change it up. Try something new. More than that, to do it long enough to effect lasting change. Forty days is widely touted as being necessary for that. Secondly, resistance is necessary. Even though it wasn't politically correct to bring that abuse to the limelight in the monastery, it was my responsibility to push back, not only for myself but to avert others being similarly treated, and to help this manager to grow. However the necessity to source my own goodness did help to free me. If I had depended on my manager's opinion of me, I would have been devastated. Instead, I remember my six months there as a fun and good learning adventure.

Yet if Anna and Michael had been with me then, it would have been different. They would have prevented the stasis of that situation from continuing. When I have difficult interpersonal situations now, we talk about it and they invariably give me simple, profound advice. The action they suggest may not feel comfortable, but as soon as they say it, I know it's the right thing to do. I can easily see, also, how Anna and Michael would have used me and influenced others to highlight to management new options for people to work out interpersonal conflict. My desire to feel valued and accepted, plus the greatest good of everyone involved, plus the beneficial work to be done by the people there for generations to come, all would have been taken into consideration. This is what I mean when I say that your desires will no longer be placed first.

The system at the monastery of balancing personal time with social interaction is, in Anna and Michael's viewpoint, excellent. However, a few pieces were missing. For example, the structure, quite formally established, didn't allow for much spontaneity. Rules about what was and was not allowed stemmed from long ago, and didn't always apply. Everyone knew this, but also knew that a structure was necessary for everyone to get things done. The common goal of enlightenment held people together, and the structure had value because everyone could play by the same rules.

Michael and Anna do not have rules. Rather than participating in an existing structure, they much prefer you to create your own, as we did at EarthSea.

Here are some guidelines for creating your psuedo-family adventure.

Create a bond of interdependence that makes you stick together through thick and thin, just like a blood family is designed to. Since that bond is not something you are born with, you have to choose it. It's best if that bond is at the level of a shared vision, and includes both spirituality and physicality. The parable of a long-distance canoe trip comes to mind. Physically, you need each other for safety. That dependence dissolves ego. Add to that an intention of working on bettering your relationships with each other, and you've got a darn fun trip. Let's go a step further, and ask Anna and Michael to join us all. Where would that go? The sky is the limit.

As you design such an adventure, you will need extra

time to jointly delineate a temporary structure. Rules will be necessary for everyone to get along; for example, on how to process conflict. Extra time will be needed for everyone to help create, and agree to, these rules. At the same time, you need to build in a process for allowing the flexibility of the moment to dictate otherwise. Both are good.

I have some experiences along these lines to offer.

Tom Brown is an expert at creating powerful group experiences. When I spent time there in the late '90s, his classes were mostly one week long, with often over a hundred people in each one. He formed us into groups of 10, and after the first day or two we felt like family.

When we introduced ourselves the first night, he encouraged us to share something deeply personal. One time I shared Michael's recent death, and the resulting tears bonded us all at the level of feelings which engendered trust. He had us all sit around a fire as we did this, and then asked us to maintain our seating arrangement for the entire week. This gave us a detailed background picture from which to enter group meditations, and fostered an amazing number of shared visions, such as one person acknowledging that he had been journeying elsewhere after someone had noticed him missing in her vision.

Tom Brown created exercises in which we needed each other physically, especially in learning to use tools and make crafts. Building a primitive fire as a team was orders of magnitude easier than alone. In Scout class, when we led raids in groups at night, he advised us to rotate leadership every twenty minutes or so. Did this infuriate the fellow who was a true scout, when an insecure housewife fumbled the direction? Absolutely. But a successful raid wasn't the point; each of us experiencing leadership was.

In fact, Tom Brown deliberately used fear, confusion and doubt as teaching tools, and they were outstandingly effective. Sending us into the night forest alone, after warning about the dark forces at work there, had some people jumping out of their skins, along with radically re-shuffling their life's priorities. Yet we all felt held by a safety net. Physically, we were within calling distance of our group members, but spiritually, we knew from our group meditations that if we were in trouble and our silent scream was loud enough, one of them would likely come running. Tom always said too that he regularly opened his awareness to spiritually help any of his students whose image came to him. Variations of these abilities to virtually help each other are part of the vision of Anna and Michael.

Tom encouraged competition. He couldn't help it; the benefit of growing up with his close buddy Rick, learning the traditional ways by playing off of each other's strengths and weaknesses, was too obvious. A close friend and I leapfrogged our learning by envying each other. For example, we decided to do a naked vision quest at the same time, going in different directions. In the dark of 5 a.m., to escape notice of the camp, we rubbed each other with ashes and clay to camouflage our bodies before heading out into the Pine Barren forest. With heightened excitement we high-fived each other as we set off. I think I can speak for both of us when I say that every bit of that (largely uncomfortable) experience was driven by the idea of staying out longer than the other. We both came back earlier than the requisite four days, burning with one question: "Did I stay out longer than she did?" To this day we are bonded because of that experience, and many others. It enhanced our friendship, because we never used it to be better than the other person, but to become better persons ourselves. Thanks, Tom, for that opportunity. To this end, Anna and Michael wildly encourage sporting and other competitive games.

A group of us decided to take the Tom Brown teachings out into the forests of northern New York State. For one week, six or seven of us were to operate as a family, not only enjoying nature but surviving in it. The fact that seventy percent of people in North America would die in a survival situation if they didn't eat meat prompted Tom to teach ethical hunting, mostly via traps, snares and throwing sticks. None of us wanted to kill anything, but we knew we needed practice if we wanted to survive the impending ecological disaster; as an incentive, we brought only plain rice and granola for food. Other constraints we agreed upon were: no toilet paper, no matches, no distractions, no tents. We shared a tarp for shelter, because in the future living in a group shelter may be the only way to survive. Our desire was to create a situation that would trigger our resistances, so that we could see/laugh at them, and then to transcend them to the point where we truly enjoyed being together. Part of this was inviting unique contributions.

Each day, one of us led the group in an adventure of our design. One fellow taught us all orienteering and led an expedition. I love blindfold work because it develops extrasensory perception. I led the group blindfolded a mile down the road to the swimming hole, assigning us each unique animal sounds to use to keep tabs on each other. Only the hunting expedition failed miserably; our only 'catch' during the week was a mouse that drowned in a rice pot left soaking overnight. Lovingly, we skinned the mouse, shared a tidbit of the meat cooked over the bow drill fire ceremoniously, and I made a dream catcher out of the skin that the organizer of the group has kept to this day.

These examples give you some ideas of how to create your family adventure. Yet other ideas will present themselves, perfectly designed to elevate your unique gifts, as you work with Anna and Michael. My vision is to live in a community of people, both families and singles, of all ages, who live for such adventures. The work of re-inventing how our society is structured starts with the family, both blood and otherwise.

Why do we not do these things at home? It's all too easy

to get caught up in routine. I speak from experience. One reason why I lived nomadically for so long was to break the tendency I have to stay comfortable in my routines. Even in a new experience, with new people, it only takes hours for new habits to set like concrete.

Here's a suggestion. Get a group of friends together, and one by one, offer an adventure idea. Listen carefully to each idea, keep your comments to yourself, and simply say, "Yes, let's do it." Then arrange a time and place to do every single one, no matter how weird it sounds, because conformity is another tendency that puts us in jail.

We absolutely need to be fresh and free to break from the past, which no longer serves the human spirit. The examples above are only beginnings. The co-creative energy prepared via joining with Anna and Michael will explosively develop ideas like these into practical, long-term living situations that are not only ecological, but just plain fun. We've set up *The Way Of Alive*™ Foundation for just that reason: to support communities world-wide that want to develop new ways of living with Anna and Michael. Check it out at **www.thewayofalive.org.**

Their vision, by the way, is even better than what we've outlined here. But first, we need to warn you: there's a cost to jumping on this bandwagon.

Chapter 14

Offer Your Life

Offer your life, and gain the world.

-Anna and Michael Christ

Chapter 14.1

Freeing Yourself To Serve

God gave us free will, which makes us powerful beyond our imagining. So powerful that God can't override our free will. That means he can only help us so much before he runs into a wall of his own making.

"Okay, I'm fully willing. I had an awesome retreat. Now I'm ready for the next step."

Did you experience contact with Anna or Michael during your retreat?

"Yes. In dreams, a lot. Also, I did have some extra-sensory experiences that told me Anna was there. I'm not sure about Michael. Plus, just by being out there, I learned a ton about myself that I never knew. I know they helped me with those realizations."

Fantastic. How far do you want this next step to take you?

"I want to go all the way. Full embodiment, as fast as possible."

Are you ready to offer your life? That is the final step to full embodiment.

"That sounds serious. What does it mean?"

Basically, it means that your life is not your own anymore. Everything you do will be dedicated to the benefit of all people. Think of it this way. You don't own your life right now. You are a piece of clay enlivened by a life force that moves through all people. This is Anna Christ. She is your enlivening spirit. It just doesn't feel that way because you were born into the illusion of separation.

"I get that, in a sense. I've often felt that when I get right down to it, all I am is a unique essence which chooses."

Precisely. When you join with I AM, you start identifying with them, and they are concerned with each of their unique essences. More and more, you recognize that you are one with everyone. This 'oneness' becomes your reference point. All your choices will start being geared toward helping others. Caring for all people as much as you do the members of your own family is the key. Don't worry, consideration and caring for yourself and your loved ones are always included. They simply don't dominate. When it comes to a choice between you and someone else, the best way to get started is to choose them. The safety net, for those of you with a pattern of over-giving, is that if your happiness, healthiness and heartiness are compromised in the process, it negates the positive effect on others. We are all one.

"I do that now, when I can. But I must admit, most of the time I'm myopically focused on my own concerns."

I understand. The next step is to empty yourself of your concerns, so that you have more room for others.

"Whoa! I have commitments I cannot ignore."

What I am talking about is not emptying the facts of your life, but the emotional baggage. That is what sucks up your life energy and makes everything take longer. Freeing yourself from that is the next step. If you don't do it on your own, and still decide to offer your life in service to Anna and Michael's goodwill for all, they will make sure it happens.

"I did a lot of that on my retreat."

I believe you. Shedding extraneous clutter is a big step in this process. Yet I suspect that you still have a ways to go.

"Yes, I admit I do. In fact, I've been working on my stuff for years, and I know darn well there are a few key lessons that I'm stuck on. No matter how hard I try, they keep repeating. If you have ideas on how to get to those, I would love to hear about them."

Anna and Michael have the best ideas. Listen to Rob's story.

My friend Rob has been aggressive in cleaning out his emotional baggage for six years, mostly using plant medicines. You will read more about how these can work in the following sections. He's been supportive of my work, and recently decided to seriously consider surrendering his life to Michael and Anna Christ. We set up a date for a commitment ceremony, both knowing that if he did decide to go for it, and if Anna and Michael agreed on the timing, they might make it happen then.

After we set the date, Rob experienced a depth of anger that was so beautiful that in my opinion only Anna and Michael could have triggered it. Bringing Rob's anger to the surface allowed them to clear out the baggage aspect of his emotion in order to purify it for his god-job. Interestingly enough, Rob targeted his anger at Michael Himself.

It started via a phone conversation we had about sexual abuse. I, with Michael and Anna, held the viewpoint that all abuse, in fact all suffering, is perfectly designed by God, or Love, to take us through our lessons. We had an argument about semantics, because Rob's definition of love did not include abuse. He understood my point of view that God is everything, but argued that if that was the case, Michael and Anna were responsible for unapologetically creating horrific suffering and needed to answer for it.

Through a series of texts, I witnessed and supported Rob through his expression of outrage, which, in my opinion, he needed to work through before he could fully offer his life. In the process, he made some great points worth sharing. Here are the raw texts; even if every meaning is not clear, you will feel the strength of Rob's feelings. I added a few comments here and there for context.

Thursday

Rob: "I apologize for arguing with you today. I'm at present sorting through a lot of pain around trespass and rape. For Michael (God) to say that what I am experiencing is really just love seems trite and disconnected at best. If this is love then I really don't feel attracted to surrendering to love."

Anna Michael: "I hear you."

Rob: "I realize that despite the fact that my Father is insensitive and out of touch, my only reason to surrender to him is because he owns me. He owns the cage I am in and all the food in the food bowl. Free will is a sign that says I can sleep in whichever corner of the cage I choose."

Anna Michael: "What a way of describing reality!"

Rob: "Am I wrong?"

Anna Michael: "No. And yes, from another perspective." I was implying that by surrendering, his cage would dissolve.

Rob: "Maybe you're just gathering up the mice he forgot to feed for the last 200,000 years, because they're starting to smell up his apartment. Maybe the reason we can't feel God's love is because he doesn't give a shit. Is this who I am supposed to be surrendering my life to? Is God going to punish me for saying this to you?"

I didn't get a chance to respond until the next day.

Friday

Rob: "Hi. Ready for round two? It's interesting why Michael refuses to acknowledge the pain we experience here, yet at the same time admits that we are so dense as to make entry impossible. Just so you know, Michael, that density is really painful. Michael and I have talked about this before. He doesn't want us to focus on the pain, because it misses the point. He wants us to turn away from it and focus exclusively on God's love. This is the only direction he wants us to look. Everything else is just learning. But that learning is f-ing painful. And to heal it we have to feel it again, which is f-ing painful again, although fascinating. His insistence on ignoring the pain by redefining it as love is insulting. Acknowledge what we're going through here. Pain isn't love and we have no perspective to perceive otherwise, because you sent the teachers home. You chose to of your own free will. Acknowledge what you did."

(The teachers he is referring to are Adam and Eve, as their story is outlined in *The Urantia Book.*)

Anna Michael: "Yes I agree and hear you. Michael hears you directly and I am allowed to say he is interested in your process a lot. I, little Anna, have the same question and the answer is slowly unfolding yet I cannot articulate it. Not yet."

Rob: "Thank you ... So after a drunken romp with Lucifer, he staggers in the door and says, "Oh my, I can't believe you're covered in your own filth. Make you a deal. If you lick it all off and then surrender your life to me, I'll let you feel my love. If you don't, I won't. Of course good luck, because this process is almost impossible, and I might not take you back anyway, and you better hurry up because I'm kind of thinking of just flushing you. You're kind of smelly and you're killing my beer buzz. This is called conditional love, and even in a lowly human I am taught that this is the wrong way to run a relationship based on love. I may surrender my life to you Michael, but not because you are a God of love, but because you are dictator and an abusive husband and I have no other choice."

Anna Michael: "You do have choice. Always." At this point, I am thinking that he must be blurring childhood memories of a drunken father with Father Michael.

Rob: "I get it. I'm stuck in your machine. I am you. But I don't perceive it that way. If this is the game, fine, I'll play. But don't f-ing tell me that what I'm feeling is love."

Anna Michael: "You sound a mite angry." I smiled at this understatement.

Rob: "No. I think I said what I wanted. Although anger is a legit emotion given my perspective."

(His immediate 'No' made me smile even more.)

Anna Michael: "Mine too."

Rob: "Denying a human's feelings is the surest way to piss them off ... I do have a choice. They make it clear. Eventually surrender your life to God, or dissolve into nothing. It's not that bad. I'm stuck in God's machine so why would I expect any other choices? It's the propaganda I find distasteful. If your other choice is eternal death. I guess that's a choice. But it's not like you are choosing between Morocco and Cancun for a vacation. It's more like the choice between eating and starving. That's not really a choice."

Anna Michael: "I am focused on writing tonight. Can we leave the texting for a while? I hope you understand. I love your thinking. It does help us."

Rob: "No problem. Do you know who gives us a choice between eating or starving? Prison guards. Love you Anna. Love you Michael. Peace out."

Saturday

Rob: "That was an interesting process to go through. I am grateful. I wonder if that was legitimate thought, or if that was just releasing fear of God? Or both? Love you."

Anna Michael: "Get ready for more adventure."

Rob: "What else am I going to do?" (He sent a smile.) "What I see is this all comes down to free will. That's the key. God gave us free will, which makes us powerful beyond our imagining. So powerful that God can't override our free will. That means he can only help us so much before he runs into a wall of his own making. Michael is right, we have to save ourselves, because essentially it is us that has the power. Actually it is us that has the power. At this point in my thought process it is this understanding of free will that is more important than an understanding that the universe is based on love because I can't feel the love of the universe. I think this terrifies Michael because he doesn't want people immersed in fear and anger to realize the power they have. A comprehension of love must come first or it could just cause more instability."

Anna Michael: "I am holding love for your process. Keep well, my brother."

Rob: "The problem is, we need a comprehension of the power of our free will in order to guide OURSELVES on the deep healing process out of the darkness we're in to feel love. Chicken and egg."

Anna Michael: "I didn't get fully out of the darkness until I was joined. The density does not prohibit their entry. We coming to a certain place in our feelings is what they are waiting for."

Sunday

Rob: "I'm not angry at God anymore"

Thursday, prior to the weekend of ceremony.

Rob: "I've always gone into any ceremony with intention. But in a way they have always been self serving. To feel better. To heal. This time feels different. Is it self serving to serve God? I'm trying to explain to Sylvia what I get out of it, and the guarantee is nothing. Long suffering? It's on the list. I see the process clearly enough. We live in God's machine. Most of my life that machine, although fascinating, has chewed me up. We are free will and that gives us enormous freedom to do what we like. But God is the puppeteer. We make agreements with him before we come here to learn and experience things. Painful things. We can't avoid these things with our free will. So in a way, free will is an illusion, even though it is real. So we surrender to the puppeteer, with no guarantees, because we see the futility of it all."

Anna Michael: "Because we love that much," (I corrected his last line from my perspective. He didn't respond.)

Rob: "I feel like God is bribing me. I know he has tricked me. It's been a weird week. Why would I do this? For I have no idea what he is bribing me with. I feel like I'm wading through mud. It doesn't make sense, but it sort of makes sense, but it doesn't. What do we do with our free will when we can see there is nothing we can do with it? Why would we trust it to the guy who's making us suffer? With no guarantees. I feel like I live inside this question. Nothing else is real. I feel like God is backing me in a corner. Showing me the power of free will, and then showing me how futile it is. Until I have no choice, because everything else is grey. I feel like I'm being hunted from the inside out. This better be going somewhere. Sylvia says it may just be another ceremony. I'm not sure what I hope for. At all. Faith. But I'm not even sure if I like that word anymore. It's like the comfort of imagining you're hanging on to nothing."

Anna Michael: "Thank you for your sensitive words."

Rob: "I'm not even really angry anymore. I don't have enough energy to be angry. I wonder. Is what I'm feeling right now the devil? What's left of the devil? It doesn't feel like personal trauma. But it's definitely at the bottom. It doesn't scare me if it is. Surrender. Who is surrendering? Michael knows. I hope he is getting some entertainment from this. Love you all."

(His statement that it wasn't personal trauma suggested to me that Michael was definitely accentuating and exacerbating Rob's anger.)

Anna Michael: "I love you too. I love you too. I love you too." (This was from me and Anna and Michael.)

Rob: "Got it. Celestial humour. Thank you."

Friday

Anna Michael: "Where are you now?"

Rob: "Want to hear something funny? In the seconds before I got your last text, I heard a faint voice in my head that said, "Can you hear me, Rob?" I said, "Yes I can, Michael." And the voice said, "Go easy on Anna." Then my phone beeped. Please add that to your book!"

I felt a swoosh of celebration. He was literally able to hear the voice that I hear!

The ceremony that weekend, Rob later said, was the most important of his life. With his intention, he formally surrendered his life to Anna and Michael Christ. During the ceremony, we (Anna, Michael, Rob and I) guaranteed our eternal lives to each other. Anna and Michael gave him his god-job, to which his entire life and particularly his recent surge of anger had prepared him for perfectly. Rob directly experienced the first levels of learning around it. Then viscerally, emotionally and intellectually he experienced a death and rebirth.

Ridding yourself of your emotional baggage is not easy. I would be surprised if you can do it alone. But don't worry. Once you give them permission, Anna and Michael will take you through whatever needs to be done in a precise and efficient way that will eventually make complete sense to you, given your god-job.

I add one qualifier. They may not get rid of all your emotional baggage, especially if it's useful to them.

"Huh?"

Have you ever felt that one of your purposes in this life is to learn certain lessons?

"Oh, yes."

Imagine that you made an agreement before you were born to learn these lessons. Does that make you feel better?

"You betcha. I have believed that for some time."

Extend that thought. Your purpose may be to learn the lesson, or your purpose may be to have others learn from your being stuck in your lesson. Maybe your gift to God, before coming here, was to offer your life's purpose to other people's learning, even if it meant you had a miserable life.

I'm not saying this is true. I'm saying that the whys and wherefores of our lessons are beyond our understanding and control.

"That makes me feel helpless. What then can I do about it?"

Do what you feel impassioned about, and don't attach to the results. Since you have read this far, I assume you feel driven to not only heal yourself, but to grow exponentially so that you can serve others. Now that Anna and Michael are with you, my advice is to pursue every opportunity that presents itself. Faith is required. As you devote your life to the good of all, your lessons will be used to help others, whether you know it or not. Eventually, whatever you are stuck on will turn into a gift that you are consciously using to serve others.

"So I just keep trying?"

Yup. Effort and decision are rewarded. Nothing you do gets lost. The love behind every single thought, word and action you take with the motive of helping yourself and others is used by your Creator parents to care for someone else. Even if you feel like you've failed all over the place, and perhaps especially so, you are gifting others. The only true failure that I can think of is to not try.

"That sounds risky. There are a lot of things I do in my life to avoid failure."

Failure is an excellent learning vehicle. We are offering you a huge carrot in *The Way Of Alive*™, an exponential growth in your health, happiness, heartiness and skills in helping others. The leap of faith required to continue means you will take what appear to be enormous risks. Anna and Michael know this, and they know how much fear we live in. Blessed be, they are willing to guarantee your safety. Read on.

Chapter 14.2

What Are You Risking?

You will be called on, at some point, to die. I found that difficult at first, and still do at times. But it's always worth it. The more you do it, the easier it is.

"You just said I can't depend on results. How can anything like this be guaranteed? People for centuries have pursued God and not found the results you are claiming here."

You think like that because that's how it's been in the past. With Christians it's the monastery, or the hermitage. With Buddhists, the three year retreat is only a beginning. In Peru, originally, the would-be shaman lived alone in the jungle for ten years. In First Nations traditions, the shaman was often the weird one in the village who lived alone. The historical wisdom is clear. You have to step away from worldly affairs, secular life, also known as samsara, to empty yourself.

Eventually, you fill up with God. You even get a new name, representing the fact that you have replaced who you were.

"I don't see that happening in my life," you say. "Not only do I have responsibilities, it doesn't sound like any fun. I've taken workshops in retreat centers. There's no sex, sometimes not even a mixing of the sexes. The food is boring and there's no entertainment. Sure, it's useful for a week. But I don't choose to live that way. More than that, I don't believe life was meant to be lived that way."

Neither do Anna and Michael. That phase of separating out the spiritual path is necessary as part of our evolution toward the integration of all things in our daily lives. Because the task of saving the planet is urgent, Anna and Michael have shortened this process so that you can clearly access their wisdom more easily. These are uncertain times, and change needs to happen fast. To move this quickly is dangerous for you, unless you have joined with them.

Because this is a brand new process, the perceived risk is high. At any moment, we may be called to a service that seems outrageous, difficult, or unmanageable. We need to practice breaking out of those entrenched thought forms that hold us back. The more we are willing to risk, the further they will take us. Helping you with your baggage, or speeding up your lessons, is only the beginning. You will be called on, at some point, to die. I found that difficult at first, and still do at times. But it's always worth it. The more you do it, the easier it is.

"I think you mean you died to a certain habit or pattern, don't you?" you ask.

Yes, and it keeps progressing. Be prepared: at some point, you may have to die to everything you think you are. You might even experience all the emotions that you would if you were to physically die. It sounds ominous, like the dark night of the soul, but with me it has been ghastly, ho-hum, and ecstatic at different times. It's a progressive freedom that comes in layers as you need and are ready for. It's part of truly offering your life.

Here's another level to consider. When you join with Anna and Michael, when they agree to become a living presence inside you, your souls are forever merged. I am told that my soul no longer exists. If you go all the way, this may happen to you.

"Yikes! You didn't say anything about that before. Well, it's a darn good thing I know now. I'm outa here. With all due respect, you are really off. Dying to who I think I am is bad enough, but to give up my soul? Not on your life."

Would you die for your child?

"Of course."

So would Anna and Michael. They take you on, when they join with you. They become fully responsible for your actions, even if you don't choose what they would choose. They will warrant their eternal lives to you. At the risk of losing you, dear reader, and at the risk of becoming a pariah to my friends, I tell you this. They will ask you to warrant your eternal life to them. That is the price they ask for their help in saving your planet.

Something like this happens when you die anyway, but it takes eons of learning on other worlds first. We are offering you a chance to 'go home' early. To become one with us now, while in the flesh, rather than growing into your own separate Christ, which is an option for every human, light years down the road, when you have learned enough.

"Well, that makes the choice clear, at least."

Absolutely.

"But what does it really mean, for my soul to cease to exist? Who am I, after that? When does this happen? How will it happen to me? What will change? Anna Michael Krista has taken your names. Do we all become Annas and Michaels, running around like little automatons, doing your bidding? Who is in charge? Why am I listening to you? I'm scared. My friends and family will disown me! This is a big deal to ask of anyone. Did Anna Michael Krista know this was the deal, when you joined with her? What did she say? How did you convince her? Is it a ruse? Is she really as happy as she claims? Does she retain her memories, her personality, the way she says? How is this possible? Why was this not stated as a requirement, at the beginning of the book? I'm not at all sure about this. You are asking me to step into something that is completely alien to me, and to everyone else I know. I've taken big leaps of faith before, but this is outrageous."

I can relate to your questions. I've had them all. This is radical stuff. What I am experiencing, and we are offering, is not something that can be explained in a casual conversation.

Writing about it is the best way to give you time to absorb the full picture, and come to your own conclusions.

I have had a lot of resistance to the fact that there's a condition of joining. Not for myself, because I was ready for it. I've also gained so much, there's no way I would turn back. I don't feel like I've lost anything. But I can't guarantee that you will have the same experience. I wish there was different way, something that still had the same bonuses, without the necessity to put your life on the line. But that's how it is.

Allow us to explain. Do this warranting with us, and you will become fully embodied. You will aid in the saving of your planet. You will die, at the level of your soul, in order to join with us. You will forever be part of who we are: your Creator parents.

Here is a softer way of saying the same thing. Let's go home now. Many of you already desire to be back in the cradle of Love you came from. This is your chance. Anna Michael Krista did not know, when we joined with her, that this would be the result. We gambled that she would be happy with our choice.

Now we are reconsidering because we feel her concern for you. In this moment, we have decided to co-create a new reality. Her soul is intact. She is no longer embodied. She will carry on with her life, as it was before.

(These words came out of me as a complete surprise as I was writing them. What you are about to read is an example of co-creation. Before this, the word 'guarantee' hadn't arisen.)

No! I'm happy now. I am honoured to be chosen for this job. I offered my life fully, long before I went to Peru, and this result is better than I ever dreamed. I stand for you, Anna and Michael. Please, I know that your stating that I'm no longer embodied is not true. But I'll say it anyway. Put us back together, please.

Done. Unless you break your vow to us, you are always with us. How do you feel about that?

I can't break my vow to you. It's established.

But you can. If you had said, "No," just now, you would have been reinstated with all your changes intact. No questions asked.

And no more dialogue?

Not at this level.

But you warranted your eternal life to me. What would that have done to you?

We would not have disappeared. We have provided for that eventuality. We will be safe, and you will be too. The person who vows to stay joined will accelerate their learning. The person who breaks their vow, will continue on the path they had before. No questions asked.

"Is there a trial period? Like a warranty? Where we can return our new selves if we don't like the fit, like at Walmart?"

Yes. Eternity. We are so sure you will like the results we gift you with, that you will always stay joined. At any time, you can say no.

This is news to me.

We saved it for now, in case we needed to co-create it. We were waiting for you to ask for it. It's a soul-back warranty. You do the work, we give the gifts, your planet is saved, (we hope), but you can back out at any time. That's how confident we are that, once you say, 'Yes,' you will stay with us. That's how urgently we are offering to help you, the ones we created, and ourselves in the process.

Believe us, this plan has been long in the making. At the same time, as we have developed with Anna Michael Krista, we have added to the plan. Adding a return policy to the warranty is one of those additions.

Is that because of my resistance to recruiting people?

Yes. We know that people are eager to join with us, as well as give us their lives. You are the one who needed this reinforcement. Not for yourself, but to make you feel confident offering us to others.

Praises be to you.

We acknowledge and accept praise at all times.

Doesn't this warranty make it too easy for people to jump in? You will get a lot of tire-kickers, the ones who put in a few weeks or months of effort and then forget about it.

True. We have considered the additional resources required. Please, also know that we are inside each person. We know precisely how clear they are in their hearts when they offer themselves to us. We react accordingly. There is a possibility for this warranty to be exercised. There is also the possibility that it won't be. You know it. You people are here, on Earth, at our request in the first place. Many of you have already asked to be of service. We now offer you a concrete action plan for that service.

Do you accept?

"I need to know more. I understand now the consequences of not accepting are that I have to give up a future as an individualistic Christ. But I still don't understand enough. If I do choose to offer my life, what would that look like?"

Chapter 14.3

The Sacred Act Of Surrender

The sincerity of my heart superseded my mind, and God's will met me in that place.

Offering your life is outwardly a simple process. You say to Anna and Michael, "I offer you my life."

Here's the catch. You have to mean it, all the way through. This is not something you can simply decide to do. You have to be ready, both from their perspective and yours. Likely you will do it by degrees, as I did.

"How can I be ready, when I don't really know what it means?"

You know more than you think. How many times have you told yourself to surrender? Each time, you are asking for a little death, a little offering of your life to someone or something else. Here's an example you might relate to.

In one of the classes at the Tom Brown school, each of us made a small staff, a prayer stick with a curved top upon which we strung natural items like stones or twigs or cloth that represented major milestones in our lives. With Tom's careful guidance bringing everyone into a sacred state, we planted these sticks ceremoniously in a field.

This was at a time when I felt guilty for many of my bad habits, for example, my penchant for Ben & Jerry's hot fudge brownie frozen yogurt. I could easily eat a pint in one sitting, and still want more.

Of course there is more that built up to this moment. But to put it simply, I fell to my knees in a state of prayer, intending to speak the words, "I commit to the purity."

Instead, the words, "I submit to the purity," fell from my lips.

The profundity of the difference was huge. Committing implied effort, discipline and forcing. Submitting implied joy, ease and relaxation. In that moment, I let go of the story that I needed to forcibly resist compulsive behaviour. I was ready for the new story that by the lure of sheer joy, the purity would propel me toward it.

In this example, I surrendered unwittingly. The sincerity of my heart superseded my mind, and God's will met me in that place. If you just say, "I surrender," in your mind, it will have a small effect. When you feel it with your entire being, Anna and Michael can change your life. Yet it's always up to both of you. Your free will is sacrosanct. So is theirs. They have a plan with you in it already. As you choose, so do they.

On the other end of the scale, you now know there are consequences for your eternal life if you choose to join with them. It may take you a while to decide to go that far. You will be tested. There is also a chance that you will not be accepted because you are targeted for a different god-job. All you can do is offer. They will decide if, when, where and how that will happen.

"If you don't mind me asking, how did the actual joining happen for you?"

The unfoldment of the actual event I have never fully described. It's too beautiful. I don't feel I can do it justice with words. I fear that others will not regard it with the sanctity that I do. I have not even been able to convey the heart of it to my dear, dear friend, who was with me and part of the experience. She didn't experience it in the same way as I did. Yet Anna and Michael, right now, are encouraging me to describe it.

It's ironic that madly, in excruciating detail, I documented all my journeys building up to this event, knowing somehow that recording the wondrous experiences of God's healing power was valuable. After I was joined, as I wrote before, Anna and Michael were leading my healing and I followed their every move. They didn't lead me to write anything down, so I didn't. Now I am left writing from memory.

There were two events, one week apart.

We were in the maloka, a round ceremony building in the healing center near Iquitos, Peru, getting ready for the shaman to pour the ayahuasca medicine. A feeling of immense sacredness descended upon me. My eyes were drawn to the circular hole in the top of the maloka, the skylight, for the longest time, as though I were looking up at God. I had had my own brew prepared, and waited to drink it until all the others had gone to the shaman for theirs and the candles were extinguished. It was about 8 p.m., long after sundown, so it was dark.

As I waited for the medicine to absorb into my system, the feeling of something sacred not only persisted, but deepened. It was a holy night. The visions began. I will describe the ayahuasca experience in general later, but it's worth emphasizing here that an ayahuasca vision is an every-sense experience. The physical, emotional, intellectual and spiritual bodies act as one. I had been in Peru, attending ceremonies four times per week, for five weeks at this point, and had also maintained a one-year diet back in Canada just prior. An ayahuasca diet involves eating extremely plain food, eliminating sex and recreational drugs, and minimizing social contact to facilitate the inner journey. So my body and heart were quite pure, except for the chewing addiction, which is a big exception.

My friend has been given the gift of singing like an angel. Lying on her mat beside mine, her singing merged into the visionary experience I was having. Honestly, I saw, felt and heard choirs of angels singing, heralding a major event and surrounding me with Love. My heart leapt toward them, revering the God that we all were in those moments. I thought I was simply being allowed to witness some magnificence, but then the vision changed. I was handed a golden thermos bottle.

A little digression to explain the symbolism. I used a thermos every day to keep my chappo, the soup made out of green plantain bananas and water, hot until I sat down to eat in my little hut. Thus it was a symbol I easily recognized as representing storing something valuable for later.

As they handed me the thermos, a voice said, "This is your soul. You are joined with us now."

The symphony, and the accompanying feelings of unbelievable grace, became even more ecstatic as these words were spoken.

Then someone handed me my little Pomeranian dog, also glowing with a golden light. The image was perfectly her, because she had that look of plaintive fear on her face that she always gets when she is in someone else's arms.

"She is a part of you now," the voice said.

Eventually, and inevitably, the vision faded and the

singing turned back into my friend's voice. She was another apprentice who had dieted even longer than I had. I knew that her pure Love had been used to beautify and enable this amazing experience.

Up to that night, in little bits at first and then with greater authority, my body had been moved by an intelligence that called itself God. Especially focused on my neck, it had been helping unwind tensions, in a precisely efficient and extremely relieving way, far better than any therapist I had been to. It had also been helping me work on others with my hands.

After a while I got up to go help a certain fellow who I had worked on before, only to discover he was no longer on his mat. On my way back to my mat, I noticed a pin light, like a single LED, glowing from the horizontal supporting beam about three feet up off the floor. Curious, because we were off grid and the generator wasn't running, I put my finger over the light and couldn't feel anything physical, like the mini flashlight I expected someone had left there. I removed my finger, and the light was still on. There is no place on the outside of the wall for a light to rest. I was no longer in a visionary state. This has remained a miracle to me.

The next morning I still felt infused with the sacred presence. I was reluctant to move, expecting that it would fade as I did, as it had with every other journey. It didn't. I went for a walk, and it walked me, encouraging me to walk in circles. I went for a swim in the local laguna, and it swam me in delightful whooshing circles. We circled around the buildings of the center, while I playfully imagined meanings, like prayers or energy clearings, in each of our stops and starts. It didn't speak until weeks later. I saw my friend at breakfast, and when she asked me about my experience, I said, with wonder, "I'm still in it."

She giggled, having had profound experiences herself. "It'll go away," she said.

"I'm not sure it will," I replied. But I didn't engage in further conversation, wanting to hold the preciousness as long as possible.

It didn't go away. Since that night, I've been graced with this presence 24/7.

What precisely happened with my soul? According to the warranty just offered, it is still out there, somewhere, in a golden thermos bottle! I realize now, as I write, that they told me my soul ceased to exist, just to stimulate my fear. To see whether I would continue in spite of that. I did.

My journeys the next week stayed amazingly sacred. But the one a week later was even more remarkable. Oh, how I wish I had a better word.

The details around the major part of the experience are vague, except I know that the sense of extreme sacredness pervaded all my journeys -- and even my days -- then.

Again I was in the maloka. In a visionary state, while communing with God as I always did, I was enveloped. What felt like a cocoon of Love was slid over my entire being. I radiated exquisite joy and my facial muscles rearranged themselves into an expression of extreme glee that I had never known before.

In those moments I became what I someday will be. I knew I was my future Self, fully *Alive* in the glory of God. Only a remnant of who I used to be was still there; when someone in my family appeared before me I felt a vague recognition, and thought, "I used to know that person. I should be able to identify them." But honestly, it didn't matter. I knew my role was different now.

I came out of that experience knowing that something magnificent had happened. To this day, I'm not sure exactly what. Did I die in those moments? Was I replaced? Was it simply a vision of who I would grow into? Whatever the factual truth is, Michael and Anna have taken me through the process of accepting, via the full spectrum of all the associated emotions, that I have forfeited my solitary life. I have lived this as a fact, as solidly as if I was hovering over my deathbed. Why? I needed to completely surrender my future to them.

"That's a special story. Thank you for telling me. I don't feel nearly ready for that level of surrender."

Don't be so sure. There are options for getting over your hold-backs faster than you think you can. You can even ask to die early, although not in the flesh.

"I'm all ears!"

Chapter 14.4

Speed Up Your Process

We can act out our stories in a visionary state, living and learning through all the associated feelings, negating the need to act them out with our friends and family.

Let's start with some background. Why are you here on this planet? There is one main reason. To learn.

This is our original plan. We splintered ourselves into little bits, which, like seeds, have the potential to become, crazily, us. We put these seeds in you and place you in a garden, a planet prepared with certain growing conditions. We set up the environmental conditions to ameliorate your growth. Then, with the exception of subtle nudges here and there, we leave you the free will to choose your paths of learning, within those constraints.

Eventually, you graduate from your planetary existence and continue your learning on other worlds.

How do you learn? Through stories. Your life is a story. Just like a book, you are the main character. You have emotional upheavals. You withstand difficult situations. You are challenged. You grow and mature emotionally, gaining wisdom. Each of you are given a few key, unique lessons to learn, and this is how you contribute to our experience.

"That makes sense," you say. "I learn best through stories. Especially the felt ones, the ones that grab my attention, move my emotions, and live inside me after they are finished."

We are talking about the kind of stories that you live through your daily life. To surrender fully, to open yourself to full service, you need to complete your stories, learning the lessons they contain. You can't fake it. You have to live them fully before you can let them go.

"How do I complete my stories?"

Think about it. Several hundred years ago, your only story was your life. Only if you were lucky did you read a book or go to see a play. The story that was your life took a long time to play out. You had one marriage, one career, and one geographic location. If you lived in a community, you learned from other peoples' stories. If that wasn't enough, you gossiped. You died feeling like you had missed something. Near-death experiences suggest that you would have had a life review, and received loving help to resolve any unfelt feelings leftover from your unfinished stories. When your slate felt clean, you moved on.

"When you talked about dying, were you talking about going through this process while still in a body?"

Yes. You already are doing so. Notice now how we are cycling through our stories with a ravenous appetite? In effect, we are living many lives in one lifetime, reincarnating as different selves every few years, or even months.. I'm sure you can relate to my stories of several long-term relationships, varied careers and multitudinous geographic residences.

This is by design. As time has gone on, humanity's ability to learn from mistakes has improved. Many lessons, collectively, have been learned and we don't have to dig into them as deeply as we did before. We truly do stand on the shoulders of those who have gone before.

Several young people I know are flitting through their stories, consciously trying new things only until they feel complete and then moving on. By the age of 23, they are having their mid-life crises, and some of them seem so wise they may never need one. The Internet and the media play a huge role in this, as well as the fact that more children are being truly cared for, so that their dysfunctional gaps are less prevalent.

"That reminds me. A group of us got together monthly last year to help each other move forward, like a mastermind group. Too often when I was sharing someone would say, "That's just your story. Write a new one." At first I was offended, but I learned to gulp it down. The point is to separate the story from the players in it, to milk what I can learn from it, and then to let it die. Re-create it with new players, a new design and plan for a different ending. It's not always easy to let go what I've invested in, but I've learned one thing. There are always more stories waiting to be born."

If we live the emotions of our stories fully, we can move through the new ones faster, to the point where at some point you won't have any left.

"But what would I do then? What would I have to live for?"

That is when you will be truly free to consciously co-create new stories, really great ones, with Michael and Anna. As long as you have unlived desires, you will be a victim of those desires. Not that there is anything wrong with desire. The only problem is when it rules our behaviour, impeding our free will.

When I was on retreat in Cape Breton, I fasted a lot, trying to eradicate my compulsive eating behaviour. At one point, I remember having a brownie in my fingertips, fighting with all my might the urge to put it in my mouth. Over and over, I had to yell at myself, "This brownie, or a spiritual life. What will it be?"

As that compulsion faded over time, it simply shifted to the bigger addiction of chewing, which became an extremely dense and heavy energy ruling every aspect my life. Much as I wanted to serve God, I couldn't because many days I could barely function. Layer after layer of disappointment in myself compounded the original problem. The tension of unfelt emotions twisted and contorted my muscles, my nervous system, my organs, and maybe even my bones.

If you had looked at me casually, you would not have noticed this. I am very good at hiding. That stuffing down of truth was another aspect of the problem.

I well knew the root of it was my story that I was not good enough. I even knew it was a story, a simple and common one at that. Awareness is half the battle, they say, but in my case it was only a smidgen.

When a friend said, "Just let it go," I felt infuriated. I had been living nomadically for some time by then, and had already let go of everything, in every way I knew how, over and over. It turned out I was incapable of doing it on my own, and none of the healers I went to were able to do it for me.

This is the case of most of us with our life-long stories, the ones we were born to live out as a means of learning the lessons we came for, and contributing to Anna and Michael's overall plan. That's why we need help surrendering. We can offer our lives in service as often as we like, and it often won't go anywhere because the freedom to change just isn't there.

"So what can we do when we are stuck like that?" you wonder.

I needed drastic measures.

It had been years since I had seen my best friend from Nova Scotia. When she said she was going to the jungle to do a ten-day retreat with the plant medicines, I decided to go with her. As a teen, I hadn't experimented with hallucinogenic drugs, and I never enjoyed the marijuana experience I did briefly experiment with. Honestly, I didn't expect much to happen from the ayahuasca. I was more interested in spending time with my friend, her new husband and another old acquaintance from Nova Scotia. But what had I to lose? For over ten years I had struggled with my chewing. Nothing.

We had to go by boat to the jungle resort. While hosted by a North American, the shamans were from Ecuador. In a beautiful outdoor pagoda, the group of us were to imbibe of the medicine on three different nights. The other days and nights were for rest and integration. The food was plain and sparse for the whole ten days. In fact on the days of ceremony we were to fast from food completely, and to stop drinking anything including water by 10 a.m.

"You are about to embark on a precious opportunity," said our guide to prepare us. "Be greedy. Drink the medicine as many times as you can. These shamans have trained for years in this ancient tradition, and will stay up with you all night. You are safe."

I took his advice. Here are some excerpts from my journal.

Tuesday: The ceremony is about to begin. My jaw has been bugging me all day. I'm due for some relaxation. A vacation with ayahuasca! On my ocean walk today I found a small stiff piece of white cardboard in the shape of a Celtic cross -- a sign that God is with me. And white! My pure heart. I wish me well on my journey. I am sincere. And I need help.

Wednesday: I got helped. She (the medicine) systematically went through my body, muscle by muscle, and relaxed it. My muscles were like jelly. I had zero muscle tension. I woke up once to what felt like an earthquake, but was a major tension release. I had lots of visuals, like Tibetan deity paintings, and then a kaleidoscope of snaking energy movement. The big teaching was about restlessness. I couldn't get comfy and kept having to change position. I got down to that root restlessness that causes my chewing, that deep underlying panic that I used the nomadic life to reach, but I couldn't stay still through it. So this is my work.

Our guide says our mind picks up the energy and paints the pictures, so what we see isn't that important. It's what it teaches us. Why then do we see so many of the same things?

Saturday: THE BIG GAHUNA HEALING. Ten years of jaw problems, with lots and lots of healings. You name it. And this one was the real thing.

At first I wasn't getting much of the visuals, just an overwhelming restfulness. Involuntarily I would sigh, letting out more big tension. A while after the second drink, I purged over the balcony, and then hauled myself up to the shaman for number three. He decided to sing over my cup for at least 45 minutes! It was only two swallows but it was power-packed. Then he had me sit on a stool in front of him and did a healing on my back. The helper led me back to my bed.

It's challenging to describe what happened next in words. I could say that I was wrestling with a snake or a panther but that wasn't it. It was a series of huge, full body tension releases. The tension was in charge, stiffening every muscle, and then progressively unwinding it, starting with my left ankle and migrating up to my throat and jaw through all sorts of gyrations ... build ups, peakings, and releasing through expelling air ... gurgling, bubbling, otherworldly sounding, uncontrollable screeching. I went with all of it. I was seeking and finding pockets and knots of tension that would travel up and, almost like a living creature, exit out my mouth.

This is what all kinds of healers have encouraged but to a scale they couldn't get me to. I don't think they could get anyone there with their one-hour-at-a-time approach. This release was so deep, it was a result of the entire week of being here.

I could sense as this was happening that another person might interpret this movement as coming from outside of me. I could build a big story around it, but really what was going on was within; kinesthetically going deep enough and staying present enough (the medicine enables this) and leaving enough time and space for the tension to unravel.

A helper mentioned yesterday that the medicine heals the body first, opens the heart second and then flowers the spirit. I can totally see this. My insides were so tangled and convoluted that there's no way spirit could make its way through the maze.

Sunday: Another mind blower! My prayer before the ceremony was for a teacher/guide. I feel ready, and I know now without a doubt that I need one.

I drank four times. Each time, the shaman filled the cup FULL! I purged within 45 minutes. Here are some things I remember experiencing.

- Seeing lots of gucky, horrible images coming up. My own stuff, obviously.
- Having 'them,' the invisible beings, work their instruments on me.
- Tension unwinding through my whole body. This started with one of the shaman's helpers massaging my neck, cranium, face and feet, manipulating what felt like bones that were not there. This magic I was then able to do with my own fingers. I spent hours massaging and moving the knots around, unwinding them.
- Reality shifting. This is the hardest to explain. Whooeee. Moving through different realities and catching up with myself. This was extremely trippy

and opened up new aspects of the universe/myself. I can say no more.

- As I was unwinding, a voice started to speak through me. Crazy words, but "upside" and "stomach" kept repeating. My interpretation is that my stomach is the root problem with my jaw, which is on the stomach meridian.
- Consistently coming back to thoughts of Love. Although I caught glimpses of rainbow-coloured jewels, I didn't really break through to them.
- Images of my body (could have been another lifetime) being cut up with knives/machetes and the bits being left in a ditch. Maybe this jaw thing came from before this life. If so, it takes the pressure off it being all my problem.

"Congratulations on that release! Now I understand why you advocate plant medicines. Is ayahuasca the only one?"

No. There are many, and different ones are used in different locales worldwide, but one aspect of the effect is always the same. A portal is opened to the spirit world through which Anna and Michael can easily perform their wizardry.

"It sounds amazing. I always disdained the use of hallucinogens, assuming that they simply produce a visual 'wow' that has no impact on daily reality. I can see now that I was wrong."

Rather than hallucinogen, I prefer the word entheogen, which means 'generating the divine within.' The potential of using these medicines to access the enormous healing power, wisdom, genius and Love of the spirit world is infinite. While everyone's experience is unique, and each single night for any one individual is always fresh, there are some common patterns.

At first, the medicine works to clear out the accumulated clutter that confuses our bodies and minds. Leftover feelings not fully lived out in our various stories arise and are purged. This clutter stems from many sources, but I can delineate two of them.

Everyone seems to have two sets of stories. One serves the key lessons that we were born with. These run deep and can be quite painful. The other are the stories we create because we don't want to face the pain of these key lessons. These are the stories of distraction, craving entertainment, blaming, acquisition, and a thousand other neuroses that stem from age-old patterns of avoidance.

Ayahuasca ceremonies systematically drive you toward clearing all of your neurosis and then getting you to understand and learn your root lessons. Experience it, and you will vividly experience the process of co-creation, because the medicine does not only do what you ask it to, what you are unconsciously ready for, and what is needed for the greater good but responds to your choices, reflexive or otherwise, in any given moment.

Most people directly encounter otherwise invisible beings on their journeys. These are all agents of our Creator parents, who are directing the show. It's easiest to reach you via plant medicines, although lucid dreaming can be an effective portal if you can achieve it. Anna and Michael can do similar things in regular dreams, but we don't typically remember them or trust them, because we are not conscious and choosing the way we are in a medicine journey.

Whatever the source of our stories, when we are stuck or spinning in them our natural spontaneity dims and our caring hearts retract. We easily and unwittingly become endlessly preoccupied with ourselves. In effect, we are ruled by our stories and thus not able to serve, create or love the way we sense that we could, if only ...

You become highly motivated to remove this 'if only' when you start working with Anna and Michael, because everything just gets easier when you do.

"Yet if they are our Creator parents, they are all-powerful. Can't they just do this for us?"

First of all, they won't just zap you to instantly fix you unless there is an exceptional reason. They want and need you to grow through your lessons, to live out your feelings, and your stories are the vehicle for that. Yes, once you establish contact with them, they will move you through your lessons quickly and efficiently, even without the medicines if that is what you choose and that is what is best. But there's a huge advantage to consciously experiencing their work, which you can in a sacredly-induced altered state.

For example, a friend of mine asked me recently if I had heard of the Christic grid. She didn't really know what it was, but I instantly did. I have experienced it hundreds of times in ceremony. It's a feeling of being enveloped in layers of delineated and woven vibrations that do extraordinary things to your energetic imprint, (or as some say, your luminous body), with a felt impact on your physical body. At times I could see beings systematically removing sections of me and replacing them. Over time, the imprint that I was born with, and had altered over time, was brand new. As a result, just like the writer and shaman Alberto Villoldo claims, I am growing a new body to match that imprint.

A lot of people have offered themselves in service. They do good things. But when it comes to making the life changes necessary to free themselves, they don't step into it fully. It's difficult. The time required, and the discipline involved, seem daunting, but witness what a two-week trip did for me.

In a single night with a plant medicine, you can live out an entire story. You can re-live your childhood traumas, substitute actions of love rather than hurt, and then be free of those old reactive patterns. You can fall in love with someone you've been infatuated with, get married, get disillusioned, end up as friends, and greet the person the next day from the viewpoint of God -- as another aspect of your loving self. You can fully embody your potential so that you *know* the form your genius takes and you won't have to wade through lifetimes of trials to find that out. You can completely experience your physical death, and come out the other side knowing, down into your bones, that it's no big deal.

In other words, we can act out our stories in a visionary state, living and learning through all the associated feelings, negating the need to act them out with our friends and family. As we have noted before, the feelings are the key. Whether the action takes place in a visionary state or with our friends and family is immaterial to the results. Progressively, we are freeing ourselves from the need for physical stimulus to learn our lessons.

"Whoa! If physical reality isn't necessary for us to learn, what can I hold onto?"

Life, learning, love and laughter. That's all I've been given as reference points. Everything else, including the existence of Anna and Michael, is just a story.

"What? You've spent all this time talking about beings that don't exist?"

Only God exists. Everything is God. Love. That is the ultimate truth. God's ultimate purpose, I speculate, is to create more Love, but individuated so that we can expand God into new realms. Expansion implies time, which God created so that we could learn how to be mini gods. How do we learn? Through our stories. Actually, through the maturing of our feelings, which happens through stories. We can't learn unless we try, and thus we make mistakes, which are highly valued. To lighten that load, God invented laughter. That is my synopsis of why we exist.

"Where do Anna and Michael fit in?"

From the revelations I've been given, and reading *The Urantia Book,* this is my perspective. Since every bit of everything is God, including us, we have a veil which shields us from knowing everything. Otherwise we would have no incentive to learn. To create and sustain that veil, God needed to create other beings who were separate from each other. At the highest level in this universe, these beings are Anna and Michael. They designed, birthed and developed every aspect of creation we know today. Keeping Anna hidden, or unconscious in us, maintained that veil. For many reasons, and only on this planet, they have now joined. As we choose and as we can handle it, that veil will be pulled back to reveal the truth of God. One reason for the upsurge in plant medicine use today is to facilitate that.

"If that's true, then what will there be left to learn?"

How to create. That's what we mean by starting life again. We will initiate the process of co-creation from the ground up, from the physical level that you exist at. What's new is migrating your reference points away from physical reality while staying in a body. Elevating your consciousness back up to a place of pure Love enables us to recreate the entire story of this planet. We are not just going to fix this planet. We are going to re-engineer it. We are going to rebuild your very existence on a foundation of putting Love first.

Chapter 15

Put Love First

What does it mean to be ***Alive?***
It means that all of your life is Love in action.
This is the promise of Anna and Michael.

Chapter 15.1

Apply The Golden Rule

We can work together to rebuild this world with loving your sisters and brothers as the motivating force of Life.

How do we re-engineer this planet? The one simple solution is for each of us, every moment of every day, to preface every thought, word and action with "I am my sister's and my brother's keeper." In other words, in every moment, in the best way we know how, we put our love for this planet and for every human being on it first. This hearty approach is the path to peace, prosperity, health and happiness for all beings.

"That sounds great, but how do we get there?"

We eradicate our primary motivation, the fear for our own survival. Therein lies the age old battle: the spirit is willing but the flesh is weak.

This has changed. You have heard me refer to Anna Christ as "Life Itself." So far on this planet, she has been hidden. She is known as the Holy Spirit, the Divine Feminine, Mother Earth, Gaia. Tom Brown's Grandfather called her *The Spirit That Moves Through All Things,* and in Star Wars she is the nameless 'Force.' She is the life energy that animates our flesh, plus a whole lot more, as she has been revealed to me. She is fully as loving and magnificent as Michael Christ, but with a startlingly new presentation of personality.

In addition to being the force that moves us, she is the creator and caretaker of physicality, of the garden in which we have been growing since time began on this planet. She has created us to evolve from animals via the survival instinct. She is the aspect of our natures that fights, competes, protects and, hidden underneath all that aggression, nurtures. All those aspects hide the power of Love. Evolution is the gradual unflowering of that Love, the natural turning inside out of our motivation for existence from 'me first' to 'us always.' Gradual evolution is no longer allowed. To save this planet, Anna has emerged.

We are here. With God's explicit permission and participation, we, Anna Christ and Michael Christ, have joined forces early. Deliberately on every planet we enact a conflict between us, a seeming separation between Life and Love. It's a playful, extraordinarily worthwhile adventure. On this planet, Earth, we gambled and lost. But only for the short term. We received special dispensation from God the Supreme to create the solution we offer you here.

Before you have learned all your lessons, we are releasing you from the constraints of physical survival. We are enabling those who join with us to put Love first.

Anna Michael Krista is not doing much more than a lot of seekers. Yet so far, freedom from physical constraints has only been enabled in rare instances, and in secluded environments. You have heard of the gurus who stay warm in freezing cold temperatures, who do not need to eat, or who move themselves through space by simply intending it.

Anna Michael Krista has not developed the skills to do these things, and yet we are asking her to behave as though she has, in a different sense. In her world as in yours, survival does not depend on those skills but on money. We are asking her to live on Love first. She has little income, and is spending all her savings to do us honour. She works by donation only. Time will prove her successful.

This is one of the primary ways we ask you to put Love first. When you decide to put your life on the line, you might be asked to do the same thing.

"Wow. I thought losing my soul was drastic enough. Now you want me to give up my livelihood?"

If you had experienced Anna Christ the way I have, you wouldn't doubt that she is capable of providing all your needs. Three conditions are prerequisite.

- You have to commit yourself to aiding their plan for the planet via *The Way Of Alive*™.
- Your god-job has to serve the greatest good.

- You have to love doing it.

Perhaps you already love what you do, or all you need is an injection of their love into what you do. If so, your means of livelihood need not change, but expect an explosive growth in the impact of your work. Otherwise, they will lead you toward a much happier, extremely fulfilling way to make your livelihood, because it will carefully develop your unique gifts.

They also aren't asking everybody to work by donation. I have that luxury right now because I do still have some savings. You will design something with them that is perfect for your situation. By perfect, I don't mean it won't be scary, or there won't be transition periods. But they will nurture you into something that will produce ease in the long run.

Personally, I need the freedom of working by donation because I cannot work by the clock. How we work with you in a session depends on your choices, moment by moment. Plus, a lot of what I do is not to be recognized as coming from me. Not having to think about money allows me to prioritize doing the right thing.

This freedom from the constraint of physical survival will manifest in other ways besides money, as will be revealed in time. These freedoms typically happen light years down the road on other planets.

Our priority is to help people develop a renewed way of living with each other, both in blood families and in bonded community.

The further idea is that everyone on the entire planet will live as though they are blood brothers and sisters.

"That sounds super scary, at least when you consider my upbringing."

Our original premise was that through your blood family, you would learn all the skills required to celebrate individuality concurrent with synergizing group potential. Then, as adults, you would be able to do this with everyone you encountered. We regret that this hasn't happened on Earth, and take full responsibility. Still, it is essentially our plan for saving the planet, along with vast technical, agricultural and other advancements.

"You mean, even though we will be freed from physical constraints, we will still have to work?"

Yes, but please release your idea of work being a chore. I remind you that this is *The Way Of Alive*™. Your work will be as *Alive* as the rest of your life, because it will be based on your relationship with Michael and Anna. They are just as interested in your work, as in any other part of your life, in teaching you to put Love first. Laughter, by the way, runs a close second.

"I hear you, but it still sounds far-fetched. I was just at a conference held by a socially conscious entrepreneur, and she specifically said to all 140 of us, "Unfortunately, you cannot live on love alone." Everyone knows that even if you have work you love, you end up doing stuff you don't want to do."

We are creating a new story. Imagine gearing everything you do in a day toward Love. Feeling it, expressing it, giving it, receiving it, appreciating it, and learning from it. Deciding what to do based on how many units of love you will give and receive, rather than how much money you earn and spend.

Why don't you do this today? The number one reason is money. Imagine that constraint is gone. Remember that for every thing you don't like doing, there is someone who does. You can now afford to pay them to do it. Plus, you get the bonus of working with someone. This makes Anna and Michael happy, because interrelationships are the best way to learn how to love.

I know it sounds crazy. But frankly, I love experimenting this way. What I have learned, you see, is that no matter how good I am at analyzing and strategizing, I can't figure stuff out nearly as well as they can. I learned the hard way.

"What's wrong with me?" I pleaded with the man I wanted most to impress.

I had done many things he had advised me to do, and spun off into many more things he approved of. Wasn't it logical that he should love me now?

He did, but not in the way I wanted him to. Then he died.

One thing he left me with was the stark truth that I didn't know how to love. That ruthless gift kick-started me into a life's journey of learning how to love, and how to give that love.

It didn't happen.

Christianity, Buddhism, Wicca, Hindu. Being one with the Earth (or, at least, trying), voluntary simplicity, living off grid. Living with people, living alone. Being in romantic relationship, being alone. Expression through dance, yoga, and theater. Long distance hiking, adventure canoe trips.

I learned that I could 'do' lots of things. Yet I could only 'be' who I was.

Unhappy.

Not all the way through, of course. I actually loved my life, full of learning, change and constant growth. The teachings I studied were wise, and I applied them. I met great people, other intensity junkies, and had fun. I enjoyed the rituals, the techniques, the experiences and the practices, but, with the exception of the solo retreats, none of them grabbed me, deep in my heart, and said, "Stay!"

Plus, I still felt awkward with people. How to serve effectively seemed always beyond my grasp. One instruction I had read stuck with me: to learn how to love, start with the plants and animals. Migrate to children and then to adults. I tried, but I just didn't feel it.

An image stuck with me of a woman I met down at the Tom Brown school. She was pinning up a notice, and the vibe of Love radiating out of this simple movement made me step back. I sensed she did this with every move she made. She loved that much.

"I don't do that," I grumped to myself. "After all these years, there's still something wrong with me. I haven't gotten to the bottom of it."

The incessant chewing both affirmed that and kept creating it.

For many years, I thought I could figure the jaw thing out by myself. Every healing session I went to was mildly therapeutic at best. Not one healer stood a chance of understanding the psycho-physiological-spiritual-emotional complex I was dealing with, let alone curing it in an hour or six or ten. As I watched my health go downhill, I deadened to hope and simply struggled to survive each moment.

"Aha," you might be thinking. "You needed an escape, and found it in those wild psychedelic journeys with ayahuasca in Peru."

Yes, these journeys reached inside me and, for the first time, touched the raw roots of my problems. As you read, within a few sessions my body released years of densely-packed emotional tensions. Yet it wasn't the medicine or the psychedelics that grabbed me. It was the Love.

My direct communication with God made me feel special, even extraordinary. Directly affirmed. Concurrent with them filling my gaping holes with Love, I became filled with a passion.

"May all people feel this way," I prayed, night after night. "I know I'm not more special than anyone else. May all people experience God in this way." When that happened, I reasoned, all the words we use to talk about what we believe in, all those words that have created not only separation but wars, will be unnecessary. Experiencing God is a much better way.

What if, instead of trying to figure it all out for myself, I had put Love first and let God figure it out for me? Rather than moving from one system to another, one book to another, one environment to another, I had stayed put, asked God to fill that emptiness and teach me how to love?

My process would have been more efficient and much happier.

Yes, my path was valid for me, and loved by God, as is yours. Yet I do not hesitate to say this to you. Anna and Michael know Love, and how to apply it, better than you do!

How can I say this so definitively?

I spent 15 years futzing around before I had those ecstatic experiences of God. Then, even after I fully accepted Michael Christ, I still had emotional clearing work to do before I felt good all the way through. Lying on the couch, offering my time, attention and willingness to plunge into uncomfortable feelings, He and Anna not only took me on deeper feeling journeys than the medicinal ones to dig out those roots, but filled the holes *and kept them filled* with so much Love that within a few short months my emotional baggage was gone.

Explicitly invite them in, and short-cut your path.

When I first started on the path of self-discovery, I dove into a 1970 classic by Arthur Janov called *The Primal Scream*, the premise being that we had to fully scream out our childhood traumas before we could behave normally.

With great anticipation, I opened the chapter called, "On Being Normal." I desperately wanted to know what 'normal' was.

The chapter never got to 'normal.' It listed many things that are not normal, but failed at describing what was. What is the natural way for human beings to behave? I contend that Arthur Janov, as almost everyone else, didn't know.

"I can relate," you say. "I've always had a knowing that there's a big gap between what we do and what Love is."

Exactly. We have this to say. Your planet was loved at one time. Then we had to care in a different fashion that resulted in you being orphaned. My apologies. But we do believe the result will, in the long run, prove beneficial. Your necessary self-reliance has created a stronger strain of independence than on other planets. This means that you are more ready to co-create ***Alive*** *because you think for yourselves.*

Meanwhile, you have been forced to live without Love as we give it. We have begun very clearly to change this world. With Anna Michael Krista, and in millions of others, we are igniting little explosions of happiness, healthiness and heartiness. Please open to the idea that you do not know what Love is at all. Then, we can work together to rebuild this world with loving your sisters and brothers as the motivating force of Life.

"Okay, help me to learn. How do I put Love first?"
Read how Sheila and I did it in the next section.

Chapter 15.2

Love Without Weird

All they wanted us to do was to feel our fear, anger and sadness, and to express those feelings. The complications we created to avoid doing these simple things were laughable.

"If I don't really know how to love, how do I put Love first? How can I believe that Love is who I am, when 90% of the time I don't see myself as loving?"

The simplest answer is to join with Anna and Michael so that they can love you into feeling good all the way through, regardless of what you are doing.

"That sounds attractive."

It is, until you do it. They make you feel all those icky feelings you've been avoiding forever, in order to uproot them. They have to be unpleasant to do this. Even when you know they are doing this on purpose, to teach you and free you, it's no fun. I can tell you it will not last, and it will be worth it, but again, when you are in the midst of it, it's no fun.

"Then why do we have to go through it?"

Because we weren't loved enough as children. I mean no disrespect to your mother, father, and any surrogates thereof. All of our parents did their very best, all things considered. Anna Christ is bringing a new level of Love to our planet that so far extremely few individuals have experienced. When I use the word Love, capitalized, this is the level I am writing about.

When you were born, you remembered this Love and sought it out in your immediate environment. It wasn't there. You grasped onto any expression of attention you could find, and called it love. Undoing the knotty associations and crooked behaviour patterns that this caused is the goal of most spiritual seekers. It was mine for two decades. It also was the first set of processes that Anna and Michael took me through via couch sessions. It seemed only natural that that was how we would help others. It starts with reaching your feelings.

One night, working with a woman named Sheila, Michael and Anna encapsulated most of my two decades of learning in a neat four hours. I pause to state that although I was working with Sheila, most everything that happened went on within me. The living presence of God in me, the images of Sheila's life that were coming to me via Anna and Michael, and my own responses and emotions carried on a dialogue with each other through my voice and body. A strong sense of the perfection of all things permeated me, and, I felt, the room also. Sheila herself spent most of the time crying, which I perceived as validation that we were hitting the nail on the head.

In the course of those four hours, we destroyed her false ego and built a new one based on Love.

Perhaps you can relate to aspects of her life story. She thinks of her childhood as average, although she has a difficult relationship with her mother to this day. She didn't party as a teen. She read *The Bible* early on, got disillusioned and married young. When her marriage broke up, she worked hard and now has a responsible management job in the corporate world. She is devoted to her kids, her steady boyfriend, and to helping her friends when she can. She is highly motivated to be the best person she can be.

With the precision of a scalpel, Anna and Michael exposed the underbelly of all this goodness. Sheila's urge toward success was really a need to impress others. She wanted her kids to be good so that she could prove to herself she was a good mother. She loved her boyfriend because she liked how he made her feel. She helped her friends so that she could feel better than them. A raging fear that she wasn't good enough drove every aspect of her life.

This emotional surgery left her lying in a fetal position on the floor, kicking and sobbing, first resisting and then fully feeling this primal fear.

Feeling this fear meant admitting she was a failure.

Feeling this fear unlocks *The Way Of Alive*™. Only by sinking into fear can you loosen it and get it moving. It might come back again, but it won't be so scary any more.

Fear just is, Anna and Michael kept saying that night. *It's an emotion we created for a reason. Being scared is fine.*

For many of us, fear isn't an emotion we were allowed to express as kids. If we weren't bad for being scared, we were distracted or ignored. Fear also isn't a feeling we associate with the perfection we are trying to achieve. Again, we don't allow it.

"But is fear Christ-like?"

Anna and Michael say *yes.*

Fear is an emotion we created, along with all uncomfortable emotions, as teachers. When you don't allow them, you don't allow us in. Feelings are the vehicles we use to help you learn.

That all feelings are fine, and the only problem is in resisting them, is what Anna and Michael seared into our very bones that night. All they wanted us to do was to feel our fear, anger and sadness, and to express those feelings. The complications we created to avoid doing these simple things were laughable. We wanted to talk about our stories, and they made us stay in our feelings. That's one way they succeeded in their emotional surgery that night. Our stories were not allowed.

Our minds -- I felt it was Sheila's, but it was also mine -- never ceased justifying, rationalizing, and creating exceptions to push away fear. I can't tell you how many times a "But, you don't understand --" got cut off as avoidance, or "I'm good because ..." was exposed as false, or "I should have ..." brought in blaming. All Anna and Michael were focused on was the emotion. The surrounding circumstances could have been anything, and were unimportant.

These ifs, buts and shoulds didn't just come through the regular spoken word. These words came out vocally distorted by fear, anger, rage, or pinned in childish tones. They squeezed out through bodily contortions reflecting the long-held clutching and perverted energy flows that create aging and disease.

Painfully, Anna and Michael drilled us into our feelings and away from our stories until in helpless frustration Sheila cried out, "Mummy!" But that only spun us into a new frustration, because our joint experience told us that Mummy wasn't going to help. In my case, my mom had simply been busy and I felt ignored. My programming said, "Don't ask for love, it won't be there." Sheila's mom had been mean, so her programming said, "Love hurts, so I better keep my claws sharpened and not let anybody get too close."

Anna and Michael were working on both of us at the same time, you see. Disallowing our stories stripped us naked until we felt the fear. But then they had to re-route it by first dissecting and then dissolving our programming. As babies, our heart strings had reached out for the love we know should be there. When it wasn't, we ended up labelling whatever approvals and attention we got as love. This set us up with cross-wired programming.

One of the associations fear brought up for me was a feeling of being trapped and my older brother 'coming to get me.' He used to bully us younger kids, and even beat us up, but at least it was attention. The one time that I resisted, because it felt more wrong than the other times, I went running to my mom with my hand in my crotch crying, "He touched me where he wasn't supposed to." She didn't respond. I programmed myself again not to ask her for help. I also programmed that my sexuality wasn't valued.

I experienced Sheila having been sexually abused by her brother in childhood, but he was her only playmate so she couldn't allow herself to call him bad. She told herself that she liked what he did to her. At least it wasn't boring. It got her things, like going to the movies. Fast forward a decade or two and she uses her talents at sex to get the attention from men she calls love. It even feels good when her boyfriend rubs her in the place her brother had hurt her.

What we call love is weird. It stems from fear.

Suppose you knew right from day one that you were a good person. That no matter what you did, no matter who you hurt, no matter who hurt you, you were still a good person. By extension, everyone you met would also be a good person. Difference aptitudes would exist, but never would you be a better good person than someone else. You could learn skills and be better at doing them than someone else, but you could never be more of a good person than you already are.

Feeling your fear isn't enough, you see. You have to replace it with this surety that you are a good person, and that that will never go away.

Good is good, repeated Anna and Michael that night. *Good is only and ever good. You are a good person. You are good enough.*

"Good is boring," came out of Sheila. "Being good is no fun," came out of me. And worse yet, "I can't be good all the time. It's too hard."

More weird programming. Feeling good is not the same as being good. The good we are talking about is the basic goodness you were born with, the foundation designed into you that transcends our perceptions of good and bad behaviour. It's not about what you do; it's about feeling good enough, at all times, all the way through. Both Sheila and I had done many good things, but we hadn't been able to feel good because the feelings of shame, rage and spitefulness that sometimes came out told us we were bad people until we got rid of them. Anna and Michael nixed that paradigm that night. Every feeling on the human spectrum is bound to, and even supposed to, come out, again and again, as we interact with others. The fact that we are good people is different from that.

Quit beating yourself up. You don't have to exercise, eat right or have meaningful work/good kids to be a good person. You already are.

"But --"

I well know it goes against everything we believe about health and happiness. But at the highest level of truth, these things are not important. At the level of living life, sure, they make for more enjoyment. But you are always, in every situation, good enough.

We need these feelings. Anna and Michael communicate via them. Fear, sadness, hatred, envy, faith, gladness, joy -- the full spectrum is needed for *The Way Of Alive*™. Monotony is not encouraged. We are scared of the volatility of our feelings only because we don't have that foundation of feeling good enough. We are also scared that we're going to sling angry and thoughtless words at another, damaging our already fragile relationships. Stop right there. Talking about our feelings is never damaging, and never something that someone else can disagree with. Stay out of the story, and stay true to your feelings, and you can easily speak your truth to anyone. Spoken in this non-violent way, anyone can handle your expression.

Dig out your long unfelt feelings, and you will reduce the chances of them whipping out sideways, hurting others. Feel good, all the way through, via Anna and Michael, and you will start to trust yourself to speak your feelings simply, and without any emotional slingshot. Preface any conversation you have about feelings, with yourself or with another, with the base phrase, "I care," and your relationships will skyrocket to a new level.

"You have done heaps of work digging out your unfelt feelings, especially via ayahuasca. But doing that scares me. After some silliness in my youth, I have always been against drugs, and I'm afraid of damaging my mind permanently. I'm also afraid of demons. Doesn't doing ayahuasca open you up to the dark side?"

That is a common perception, especially for those who operate at the level of good and bad. It's true that scary experiences happen on an ayahuasca journey. Their purpose is two-fold. One is to bring to the surface your own unfelt feelings, and if you have repressed them for a long time, you may project them into what appears to be a very real dark entity or a demon. Once you have cleared yourself from those pent-up emotions, you may be asked to go a step further, and keep clearing unfelt emotions that Anna has stored away.

"Anna? I thought she was Christ?"

Please accept this simplification. She is the force of Life in all creatures, deliberately separated from Michael Christ, the force of Love, on this planet when life began. This separation was required to evolve the species through the process of natural selection. Survival, the focus of the critter brain, dominated Love. The resulting fear and suffering has been collectively held by Anna in abeyance.

"What does that mean?"

She has held the unfelt feelings of all people on earth for all time. Each new generation of people has carried, both physically and emotionally, those bent, compressed, and perverted feelings of anger, sorrow and fear. These feelings have necessarily been expressed by Anna in distortions of the physical body, disease, pestilence and horrific acts by individuals.

"You mean she deliberately created suffering? How can that be Love? How can that come from God? I feel betrayed!"

She, and the fact that She's been hidden, is the reason why God has always seemed to be speaking with a forked tongue. On one side, goodness and love. On the other, suffering. Since time began, people like you have been yearning for a Love they know is true, and Life smacked them in the face. God created Life. How can anyone trust a Love that created suffering? A big part of this work is understanding why this is, and forgiving God.

Chapter 15.3

Forgive God

Understanding that Anna has been inflicting fear and suffering on you, and on the entire human race, for the sole purpose of hacking, carving, burnishing and finally polishing you into a Christ will help you forgive Her, and in the process, all of God's plan.

"My father said that God had a use for all that suffering," you remember. "That there was a Divine plan that somehow made it worthwhile. He had a lot of faith, but it wasn't easy for me. I just got angry. Now I know why."

Faith has carried people through the suffering that they didn't understand. Many think that experience is separate from God, that God is in heaven only, except for the odd miracle. Or that we have to step off the wheel of samsara to get to nirvana. I am telling you that every bit of your experience comes from God, and that becoming god in a body is a descension rather than the ascension we've all been waiting for. It is not separate from Life Itself.

"How is that possible?"

I offer you the explanations given to me.

Anna is Life Itself, the progenitor of all of our experience. She has used the fear of survival and physical/emotional suffering for one purpose: to grow the species. She has pitted us against each other physically so that only the strongest, fittest survive. She and Michael have denied us the Love that, in the deepest parts of our hearts we know is real, and then kicked us about with trauma and disease in order to grow us emotionally. They have veiled us from truth, forcing us to both create the reasons for our existence and then to angrily debate whose creation is real.

"No wonder I don't trust God."

I understand. I have felt betrayed many times.

"How can you live with yourself? Promoting something that comes from a force you admit is manipulative, and even cruel?"

Because I have experienced the end result. Let me continue.

Life has always been a conundrum. I heard a typical comment about this today. When I asked an acquaintance why they looked so tired today, she sighed, "It's just life. We've all got one." Many of us have given up on trying to explain it, and focus instead on accepting it. Here is my attempt at trying to lift a little mist from the mystery.

We are born into challenging circumstances with one all-powerful tool: free will. Life happens, and time and time again we are given a choice as to how to respond. We do not control our environment or others, and often we cannot even control our feelings. Yet we choose our thoughts, words and actions. With each choice, we are learning how to be a Christ, one who is able to wisely and mercifully adjudicate and forgive. To get to that perfect state, we are being progressively purified though the forge of fear and suffering. When I say 'we,' I mean all people who have existed for epochs, because concurrent with individual progression has been the collective progression of humankind.

This straightforward process -- to come to this planet with a carryover of unfelt feelings and unlearned lessons that will be manipulated through life events by Anna Christ until we choose freedom from emotional suffering, which means we've learned our lessons -- has typically not been completed by single individuals in one lifetime. When we die, we are given a life review. We see the big picture, and are lovingly held until we understand what the impacts of our thoughts, words and actions have been. Then we move on, and keep learning. What happens to the mess of unfelt feelings, and the remnants of unlearned lessons, that we leave behind? They are happily received by Anna, who then propagates them into the next generations. This is one way of looking at evolution.

Not being able to understand this process until after we are physically dead has made it harder. The only thing we have been able to hang onto is faith. Somewhere, somehow, many of us have had the inner knowing that whatever we are going through has a purpose.

The time of relying on faith alone is over. Experience is displacing faith. One good plant medicine journey, for example, will prove to you that there is life beyond this 3D reality. No more need for intellectualizing or hoping.

With it becoming obvious in recent years that you can complete lessons while in your current body, you can expect to, if you haven't already, applaud all the suffering you have gone through because it has created your unique gifts. Most people like me, who have come out the other side of horrible suffering, say that in retrospect they wouldn't have had it any other way.

Anna Christ is relieved. Finally the hidden purpose of her thankless job is being revealed. Understanding that She has been inflicting fear and suffering on you, and on the entire human race, for the sole purpose of hacking, carving, burnishing and finally polishing you into a Christ will help you forgive Her, and in the process, all of God's plan.

"I thought you said Anna Christ was full of Love."

She is. It simply manifests so apparently fragmented, confused and peppered over millennia that it has been unrecognizable. Her job today, revealed, is actually the same as it's always been, in purpose but not in form. Instead of acting out our lessons on the people and things around us, we are offered the chance to act them out only on the emotional plane. Here's an example.

Last week I was thwarted from writing this section. Anna and Michael kept me pinned to my chair, unable to write, unable to choose any other action, and physically feeling suddenly ill. I had a deadline, and knew what I wanted to write. Why wouldn't they let me? I felt extremely frustrated, confused, angry and impatient. They wouldn't even let me stop trying!

They were taking me through a deep and condensed experience of impotency. Frustration at not being effective in serving others over the years has stimulated a lot of impatience in me. To prevent me eagerly forcing *The Way Of Alive*™ on others, they took me through this expression of impotence so that I would accept their Divine timing. I know this because since then, I have felt a supreme serenity and blessed contentment. I now marvel at how significantly this lesson changed me, over such a little concern. Yes, I suffered painfully, but in the scheme of things, failure to meet my deadline is a trivial event. It's not physically painful. It's embarrassing and emotional, but it is not harmful. It doesn't affect people in ways that truly damage them; only their opinion of me is in jeopardy.

"Why were you physically ill?"

It was an effective way to keep me from working. Another reason is that they have been upgrading my body, and this was a good opportunity to do some concentrated work. They work in layers, so I'm sure there are more reasons, but I don't need to understand them all. I do have faith that it was useful. It's a faith built on experience: every time I have struggled, the results have been excellent. No matter what Anna and Michael do, I know they are doing it with love and with the greater good as their objective. One background constant lesson is quite simple. Love anyways. Whatever is going on, no matter how debilitating or incomprehensible, from them directly or from them working through others, find a place of loving anyway. Even though, despite and in all ways, choosing to love -- which doesn't negate all the other feelings, but rather embraces them -- is the challenge, the teaching and the lesson.

To sum it up, Anna is an expert at manipulating the forces and events of life to create our perfect lessons. She is offering to do this for you faster, with clarity of purpose and the satisfaction of an understandable result, long before you die. When this happens, I can say from my experience that you will bow to her in praise.

"I'm not so sure about praising Her. You've been talking a lot about co-creation, but when you were pinned to your chair, there wasn't much of that going on."

In some ways I have co-created. In other ways, I'm not wise enough yet. It happens by degrees. Let's face it; I am a puny human and Michael and Anna are perfectly good. They invite me to co-create selectively, only when either my desire is clean of 'me first' or when my 'me first' suits their plan perfectly. But I will give you a hint about co-creation.

Anna is the master manipulator, as I said. She's been doing it for the good of a distant future, but that future is now within our lifetime. The idea of manifestation that you've been exposed to is like tiddlywinks compared to what she is capable of. What she's been doing underneath your conscious awareness is now available with the express cooperation of your free will. Michael's too, and that's the safeguard. He is Love, which encompasses decision combined with wisdom, mercy, fairness, and a bunch of other things. He chooses which manifestations are allowed.

The experience I am gaining by giving them full permission to help me work through my stuff however they like, which has been difficult, ecstatic, and everything in between, will be fantastically useful when I am clear enough to co-create actively with Anna. In learning how they work with me, I am learning how to work with them in the future.

"I feel scared," you say. "When you talk about manipulation, I think of the dark forces that unsavoury people manipulate. Witchcraft, voodoo, black shamen. I'm sure you encountered stuff like that down in Peru. Where does evil fit into all this?"

I have encountered many dark visionary experiences while in Peru, even ones that I saw coming at me directly from other persons. In a visionary state, you can perceive dark imagery or scary sensations, eyes closed or eyes open. What your mind does with those perceptions is extremely creative, taking you through new/deeper feelings and teaching you about how your mind works. In all cases, the underlying force is Anna releasing unfelt emotions.

"I have heard of abuses by shamans who aren't anywhere near their victims. How does that work?"

My relationship with God was my protection from the abuses of dark shamans. Concentrating on and developing your own goodness, combined with building a relationship with God, fills your gaps such that malevolent intentions don't have anyplace to land and boomerang back to the originator. Thus I do not have a story about that kind of shamanic abuse. But this is what Anna and Michael have shown me. Anna, who often manifests darkly, is the power of creation. In my experience it is a beautiful and clean darkness, like the earth, like compost. This power can be used to create good or deliberate evil. Ultimately, since She and Michael are in control of everything in this universe, there is a positive effect of all abuses; Michael has allowed them, although it may take generations for the reasons, and the results, to become evident.

Dark shamans have learned, via explorations in non-physical reality, to harness some of the powers of Anna. They execute a choice to use that power for evil. They may think, at some level, that they are doing good. Regardless, they are exercising their prerogative as a free willed individual and it may damage another, unless they call on God or Christ.

Michael is the divine arbitrator, who sees all past, current and future consequences of any action. If He is called, He will determine whether any attempt to use Anna's power is allowable based on the good of all concerned. If He is not called, then the responsibility for that judgement is taken on by the shaman who chooses. The result of that judgement, and of any actions taken, and the fate of that individual, will be determined by Michael with mercy and fairness.

In my case, I can say with veracity that in addition to resurrecting unfelt feelings, Anna created the dark situations I encountered deliberately to develop my character. Would I choose to love God anyway, even though 'He' allowed these scary situations? Would I shun, criticize, slander or otherwise complain about the individual involved, or would I take the high road and simply say, "I don't understand, maybe it didn't come from him/her at all but was a projection of my own unfelt feelings." Such demonstrations of the vast and incredible untapped powers of the human mind to create reality are extremely instructive.

At another level, these experiences drove me to seek God for refuge. The more I resisted the dark imagery, the stronger it got, and the more love for God I had to generate to survive. I could have stopped at any time, and said, "This is too much evil. Someone's got it in for me. I'm outa here." I'm glad I didn't, because I have since lovingly been guided to see Anna's dark power for what it is; all the benevolent, wise, nurturing, bounteous blanket of goodness that you imagine Mother Earth to be.

The earth itself is not a spirit. The capacity for growth is, and it is Anna. She is the active expression of God, responsible for creation. Her powers, and the concurrent potential for rapid change on Earth now that She has emerged, are beyond imagining. For example, one hint I have been given is that she controls gravity. This means she also controls anti-gravity. Inside these two things, I am told, is free energy. Are you the one she will co-create that with?

Think about cancer, the potential for rapid growth in the body. It would have taken centuries for us to figure out how to harness that capacity for growing new bodies. Now, she will share that information via anyone whose god-job it is to develop it. She has created every disease with the objective of developing a new aspect of life. Believe me, she understands health and the intimate connections of the human body. She created it. Everything She has created on Earth is ultimately good. She works completely with, and is as good as, God.

I, Anna, am ecstatic that my consort, Christ Michael, has decided, in all fairness, to return to Earth. Now we get to complete many of the projects we have been working on for ages, and start Life again. I have the mandate to create new children who are not only physically free of the carryover of unfelt feelings and lessons from prior generations, but free from the critter brain, the aspect of your psyche that fears for your physical, emotional and intellectual survival. No more will competition kill. These children will automatically view games as win-win, fun, skill-building opportunities. Compassion will be at the forefront of their decision-making. Beautifully, for those parents who have chosen to join with us, and then procreate them, these children will be born joined with both Michael and I. As they grow, they will be taught by us the simple truths of how God works, of the way we, their Creator parents, have structured the operations of this universe, and they will also have, as their friends and teachers, the helpers that have been mostly invisible to you.

"Fantastic. But you said 'in all fairness.' What did you mean?"

You humans have borne the brunt of suffering without knowing why. With this return of Michael Christ, via anyone who joins ***The Way Of Alive***™ *and other means as well, you will very quickly understand so many of the whys and wherefores of our actions that we pray you will forgive us.*

It's almost as though to balance out the extremes of long suffering, they are going to give us a huge wallop of goodness. The basic frame of this goodness is established. Yet, how we fill that frame is still to be determined. They have plans, ideas, which are potentialities. They test these potentialities on us via stories: which ones do we choose to believe in, to feel good about, to allow into our lives? The choices we make will solidify one of the versions of the future they have created.

Eventually, because of the perfection of all things that they are, we choose the version that they prefer. I'm not sure how this works. They have created their version, and delicately they weave us toward it to the point where we think we have chosen it ourselves. It's the magic and profound intersection of destiny and free will.

In this case, the destiny we have chosen, unwittingly, here on Earth, is phenomenal. We have suffered enormously and our planet is a mess, but it's all been for a greater, higher, exalted purpose that even *The Urantia Book* did not portray. We, the beings on this planet who say, 'Yes' are to be the co-creative progenitors of a whole new experimental existence. I can say no more right now. I do know that I will be writing more books as this revelation unfolds. I do know that since Anna and Michael have openly joined together, life on this planet has changed permanently and for a huge amount of good. When you know this, which you will discover in your own way, you will forgive God too.

Here's another way of thinking about it. Good is the foundation in each of us, but it hasn't had the power. Self-interest has been the force that has created our ways of living. Anna is that power. Now that She has emerged, She can use that power openly to leap us forward by taking survival out of our thought processes, after we join. She can now accelerate our lessons openly, with our cooperation, without having to spend a lot of resources manipulating life events to do so. Instead, She will manipulate life events to directly support the return of Christ Michael to Earth. The power buried in what we used to consider Darkness is charging forth with unstoppable health, happiness and heartiness in this harmonic convergence of Life and Love. Regardless of whether you believe my story, please trust that the future is bright, very bright indeed.

Don't get ahead of yourself though. There's a whole kit bag of tools at our disposal that we have yet to learn how to use. May you laugh as you learn how to use them.

Chapter 15.4

Love Your Mistakes

You are a baby Christ.

"Wow," you exclaim. "I am so moved, I am filled with gratitude. I offer my life. But there's a big gap. I don't yet feel this Love you are talking about. How do I get started?"

You do what feels good.

"But how do I know that what feels good to me is what Michael would choose? How do I know it's not just self-serving?"

Joining with Anna and Michael provides a safety mechanism. You have complete freedom to do what feels good to you. Whatever you do, once you join, will be perfect. It's like there being a smart safety catch on a gun. If you shoot in the wrong direction, the gun simply won't go off. The power you intended will, likely, boomerang back to you as a lesson. If you shoot in the right direction, you will feel good right away.

Then there's the in-between. This is where you do what feels good, and the immediate effect isn't what you expected. You may even feel awful, like it was a huge mistake. Trust me, it's perfect. You have been encouraged, through feelings of goodness, to do something that needed to be done to progress the plan. Layers of perfection will unfold over time. It was a perfect lesson, or trigger, for the people you affected. It was a perfect demonstration of your neediness, the parts of you that are still myopically self-serving. It was designed to whip you into shape, for your god-job, without the sting of judgement. Hurrah!

If you are living, you are making mistakes, in the way that you are designed to. You are being carved into the perfect performance of your god-job. With the genius of Anna and Michael, the very carving is your perfect contribution. There are consequences to your behaviour, but there is no retribution. You are free.

Life lives to feel good. We do everything to make this happen. This is a holistic affair. In it, you are a baby Christ. You may perceive perfection, and then find out you've made a mistake. Whatever it is, it is to the benefit of both your/our soul and mankind. Please do keep that in mind.

"That sounds confusing."

Yes. It certainly confused me. I'm hoping this story will help you.

Before I was given the name Krista, Michael and Anna kept telling me I was Anna Christ. Naturally I didn't tell anyone, and I resisted believing it. Yet there was evidence that I was a Christ in the making. When I worked on myself or others, my fingers moved by themselves, and my voice spoke love, instructions and unexpected words with a crystalline resonance and perfect timing.

I didn't have a history as a healer, so I started working on people for free. When I held a session, I turned myself over one hundred percent to the divine presence within. I felt honoured to offer many of the teachings that I had worked through already.

My friend Christine had multiple challenges in her daily life. Environmental sensitivity kept her home alone, or rushing home sick from events where other attendees had done something as innocuous as washed their hair with a fragrant shampoo. She had had a brain surgery that limited her vision so that she could no longer drive. She had many gifts, and she burned with frustration because her physical situation kept her from pursuing her dreams. Yet her presence was, and is, always fresh and bright, and she has the gift of truly comforting strangers with her biblical faith in Christ. I had told her that I worked with Christ, and offered to help her.

It was a perfect healing session.

She lay on her bed such that I could work on her head. I heard her muttering prayers and joined in, hoping to help her relax. I knew she was scared, because she had told me many times that pastors had warned against alternative healing practices. I verbalized the power of, "When two or more are gathered in the name of Christ," and finished by asking for her highest good. Love infused me and moved my fingers over her cheeks.

"Beautiful lady," spoke Michael and Anna, using my voice. They moved my fingers delicately. I felt surges of energy flow into her, and jumping spasms as tensions released. Verbally, Michael and Anna honoured her kindness and told her how bright a light she is. My left hand anchored into a spot behind her left ear, and my right hand centred on her heart.

"I am very, very, very loving and you are alive," we told her. "You are a Light. You are God. God wills that you are healed. Prayer is a blessing of God. And now we pray. You are beautiful and you are alive and I am the breath of Life. You are blessed." My head bent close to her heart as we whispered these fully embodied Words into places that needed them.

Then came a surprising instruction. "Tap your fingers. In preparation for your healing, tap your fingers on your head. A lot. A lot. A LOT." She started, and we affirmed that she was doing it right. Although this surprised me, it made total sense. Tapping would start activating life force, an intention to heal and draw blood flow to her head to heal the injury.

I stood back up and my fingers went to her left eyelid. What felt like electricity charged into her for several minutes, and her eye responded with rapid pulsation.

Then Michael and Anna spoke about her paralysing fear, naming sheer terror and murderous hatred leftover from severe childhood trauma. Prior to this, Christine had said that her brain surgery had left her unable to feel her feelings; we tried to tell her that she was simply terrified of the power of her unfelt feelings, and that feeling them would be necessary in order to stop her from unconsciously projecting them 'out there.' I sensed that the chemical sensitivity, at a deep and uncontrollable level, gave her a shield from the slights and often unconscious insults that people habitually sling at each other, which she is extremely sensitive to.

Telling her this at the level of the intellect did not feel effective enough.

"You are f–ing terrified!" came out of my mouth vehemently, I assumed to trigger her into a reaction.

I don't like this word, but Anna and Michael had recently been forcing me to say it, to get me over my reactivity. Aversion creates separation, and God is everything, both good and bad. The bad is an opportunity for new growth, and hence is always good. Taking this newfound teaching forth, and riding on the perfection I felt in speaking it, I allowed it full impact.

She didn't respond. With me feeling slightly disappointed that no tears or emotional breakthroughs were forthcoming, we soon wrapped up the session with nurturing reassurance.

"You are very scared, but fear is fine. Fear is *Alive*. Life is feeling. All feelings. All."

I felt enthralled with this complete healing package that included bits of acupuncture, cranial sacral touch, prophecy, psychology and prescription. Not to mention the direct blessing, the Word that God was willing her to heal. I praised Michael and Anna for allowing me this ability without having to train. When Christine sat up I asked her what she had experienced, expecting awe and wonder.

"Not much," she stated.

"What?" I exclaimed, my eyes wide with disbelief. "You didn't feel the energy coursing through you?"

"Nope."

"It didn't mean anything to you that that God is willing you to heal?"

"I didn't understand what that was all about."

Unbelievable. Those words came through me crystal clear, with sacred resonance and good grammar. What was there not to understand?

"Did you get it, that you are to tap your head to prepare for your healing?"

"Oh, you mean I should still tap it?"

It was as though we hadn't been in the same room together.

"You don't believe that God is with you, that He wants you to heal?"

"You will have to believe that enough for both of us," said this evangelical, prayer-habituated woman.

I went home stunned. I knew the stellar quality of our session. At the very least, it should have been therapeutic. I felt it could even have been curative. What was blocking it? The only answer was that her fear -- of me, of me saying I work with Christ, of me telling her she was God, of her own healing perhaps -- created such a shield around her that nothing, not even God, could get through.

Tell her she is fully healed, Michael and Anna told me. *Tell her you are Anna Christ, and that she is fully healed.*

Was this a test of my faith? If I dared, would it be true? Was instant healing within my grasp?

"Really?" I gulped.

Yes.

It felt worth my embarrassment to text this message to her, just in case it worked. It didn't heal her. She politely responded her thanks, and continued to suffer.

It took me some time to summon the courage to ask her more about it. It turned out she had been put off the session completely when I used the F-word.

"It's very specific in the Bible, not to use blasphemy," she said gently. "When you used that word, I knew it wasn't coming from God."

She never let me work on her again.

Allow me to catalogue the litany of mistakes I made in this session, in the hopes that you can avoid some of them when your skills accelerate.

First of all, I completely abdicated responsibility for the session to Michael and Anna. They had been telling me to co-create with them, but the gap between their capabilities, and what I could do without them, was cavernous. I was so starstruck, I abandoned my basic personality, the one that likes to please and is even tentative at making strong statements. I ignored the respectful practice of asking Christine what she wanted worked on, or telling her what to expect in the session, or even getting her permission to do what I did, and I didn't check in with her as we went along. Where was my basic human respect and decency? Lost in my hubris. That's just the first part of the list.

I was new at this healing game, and, frankly, eager to share what I had gained to the point of railroading Christine into the healing I thought she needed, the feeling kind that I had had. Michael and Anna charged this neediness in me, making it come *Alive* and making me feel perfect while doing it. For example, when I wanted her to break into tears, they brought out the f-word. Why? To teach me, feelingly, the consequences of me thinking I knew what had to be done. I lost the trust of my neighbour. Ouch!

Thirdly, I was rushing my god-job. I had this gift of working with my hands and voice, and wanted to use it. To me, any sort of healing work was worthwhile. But Michael and Anna are much more precise than that. It took time for them to develop the backdrop of why I would do this work, and how, and when. It turns out that using my hands and voice to channel healing energy and information is not my god-job. My god-job is to help you learn how to receive healing and information directly from them.

Fourthly, I wanted instant healing, without regard for the bigger picture. Perhaps she had not learnt all the lessons her pain was there to teach her, or perhaps the statement 'God is willing for you to heal' was for the benefit of my hubris, or not meant to be absolutely true yet. I also wanted it to come through my hands. Michael and Anna do not work that narrowly.

A few days after this session, Christine noticed a poster about a work program, which led to a healing program, after which she said, "I feel better than I have in years." Since then, various new levels of happiness have come into her life. While our session had something to do with it, it has, I suspect, much more to do with her years and years of fervent prayer, and the timing that Michael and Anna have in mind for developing her gifts.

Lastly, I must say that while this session was a colossal mistake on my part, it was not a disaster in the least. The perfection I felt during every aspect of that session was true; the results were simply not what I was expecting. Christine and I have, surprisingly, stayed friends. In fact, some time later she casually mentioned that she couldn't remember what had bothered her about our session. I now trust that I can make mistakes and people will like me anyway.

I don't know the whole picture, but I do feel strongly this session was an integral part of a delicate weaving of our lives working together and helping each other. For example, I am still learning from my frustration when she stubbornly, it seems to me, doesn't do what I think she should do to help herself. To see that she is totally being directed in all she does has been difficult for me, but is being revealed. Since that session and other mistakes, I have relaxed my charge to help others whether they need it or not. The luxury of resting in the knowing that all will happen as it should is slowly permeating my experience.

Faster than I did, I hope, you will learn to cherish your mistakes and even relish the opportunities to make them. Take the risk, I encourage you, especially once you have joined with Michael and Anna. The drama, or the physical consequences, will be less than you think, and eventually the crushing feeling that you are a bad person for making them will pass through more easily. You won't escape the stage of repentance, however; that is necessary for you to feel good about yourself, all the way through.

For a long time I thought the spiritual path meant being affirmed supernaturally that I was on the right track. Love, and developing a clear intuition to use it, was my goal. I see now that while Anna and Michael applaud such a lofty goal, the true measure of progress is the straightforward character development that comes from taking action. Courage, teamwork, discipline, compassion, integrity, wisdom, patience, independent thinking, honesty, fairness and other traits take effort, mistakes and time, but that's where we ground the Love.

"That sounds like a grind."

It isn't. Not with Anna and Michael. They imbue me with such zest, wrap me in so much love, advise me so well along the way, and joke with me so much, that I don't think about developing these traits. It just happens, especially when I serve others.

Chapter 15.5

Serve Others

Service, on the scale that Michael and Anna are talking about, is far more than giving money or time. It's giving everything you have of yourself to the betterment of Life Itself, which rests in the development of the divine children.

"You keep talking about helping others," you say. "But honestly, I spend so much time on myself and my loved ones, it feels like enough. Why should we do more?"

Good question. We all know we 'should' do more, and I bet you give money, and even time, when you are directly asked. Why? Because there is an emotional appeal to your heart.

"You are right, but here's the truth. I give at those times because I feel guilty for not giving more."

Then there's something that doesn't feel right about it, correct?

"Yes."

That's because the 'should' is a fallacy. Ultimately, giving comes from a burst of caring in the heart. It's spontaneous, natural and, ideally, a creative response to any unique moment. Somehow, in our occidental culture in particular, that naturalness has been programmed out of us. Spontaneous trust in reciprocity, even with our own siblings, is weak.

Our animal instincts tell us to look out for number one. With Anna and Michael, your number one is enlarged. You are, we are, I am, one being, God, splintered into billions of different aspects. Let go of the 'should.' When you join with them, you will start treating each of those aspects as just as important as yourself. Who you help, when, and how much will depend on your god-job, which gets defined after you join. What you end up doing will be precisely what you enjoy doing. Reassure yourself that you don't have to do it all. Luckily we who join will all be working with each other.

"Hmmm. What about the fact that when I work with others, we often clash, especially when we have the same issues."

I found, when living in community, that at least one person was always bugging me. Curiously, who that person was shifted. What was bugging me about one person would fade, and something else would crop up in someone else. The bugging just moved around. It was all about me. We all came to the conclusion that we were simply working through each other's issues as we worked through our own.

"Sometimes, though, they aren't working on their issues the way I am. They just focus on my issues! Then I get doubly irritated, and make things worse by having my anger come out sideways."

I've worked with Anna and Michael for a while, and seen a lot of benefits that will be extremely valuable to all of us enjoined ones who choose to live together in community. If my words don't come out cleanly, with a solid resonance, I know I'm on the wrong track. Sometimes I'm explicitly prevented from saying something that's a little off, for example if it has a tinge of gossip or judgement in it. A few weeks ago, while talking to a new acquaintance in the healing field about our respective paths, I was about to suggest that a plant medicine ceremony might help her but I wasn't allowed to. I sat with my mouth trying to work and physically unable to get any words out for close to a minute. Laughing at my own spectacle, I wondered if it was because talking about the plant medicines would be too radical for her. It wasn't. As thoughts kept spinning words through my feelings to see which ones were right, the ones about being embodied fell out. I didn't know it, but Anna and Michael did. This woman had been developing a strong relationship with Christ on her own, and was fully ready to say, 'Yes' without ever having been prepared by me.

Anna and Michael help in many ways, and use us to help each other too. They can work anyone's issue through anybody else, which especially might happen within the group of us who have joined. Let's say Anna and Michael decide to work extra hard on a certain subject. For example, they want to bring through new kinds of babies, and they need our belief structures to open up to the idea that it's possible. Last year, they made me believe that I would have one. I'm technically too old, but I went with the experience, because I knew that my feelings of being thrilled, and believing it was time to birth a divine child, would help them to bring it through whoever ended up being the one(s) who had that god-job.

"You mentioned living in community. Are you talking about a group of people sharing everything, including livelihood?"

At first, Anna will provide for our livelihood. Over time, we will develop many revenue streams which will require teams of various composition. We will also work together tending gardens and animals, but I expect each family will have their own abode. These are bits of the vision they have shared with me, which are congruent with the ones presented by Anastasia in *The Ringing Cedars* series of books. I have no idea how we will get there.

"What scares me about that is the idea that one person won't pull their weight. Even if money is not involved, this can be a real irritant."

My first answer to that is not to worry. Each one of us will need to take time out, to work on our personal relationship with Anna and Michael, and to develop our god-job further. Like the maestro of an exquisite orchestra, Anna and Michael will ensure that all aspects of our work -- on ourselves, on each other, in our homes and on the land -- will be *Alive*. In other words, our work will be wondrously integrated by them for the long term benefit of all. It will not be perfect right away, from our immediate perspective, and we will make lots of mistakes as we grow. But remember, learning how to profit by every individual's unique contribution to the whole is a huge part of Anna and Michael's motivation. Developing sisterly and brotherly love will not be an edict that comes down from on high. It will become natural. No one will be left out.

Now let's step back for a moment. We are designing this community together. No rules will be made, or structure developed, by any single individual. All will be coordinated by, and aided enormously by, the divine wisdom of Anna and Michael coming through each of us. They will be the bond that holds our community together, and our lifestyle will be determined by how we co-create with them.

This bond will naturally evolve to stimulate each of us serving the other, for the good of the whole. Service, on the scale that Michael and Anna are talking about, is far more than giving money or time. It's giving everything you have of yourself to the betterment of Life Itself, which rests in the development of the divine children. The Iroquois edict to provide for goodness seven generations down the road is expanded by Michael and Anna to be many generations, and more than that. They want life on this planet to be turned inside out. From a mess, it will become not only sustainable, but enjoyable and fruitful, on all levels, for everyone.

These last two thousand years, Anna and Michael have carefully been expunging all the unfelt feelings that on a normal planet they would have held as teaching tools for the future generations of humankind. That's why since the time of Jesus life has been dark, dark, dark. The new breed of human will be born without any unfelt feelings from prior generations. In addition, they will not carry the animal fear of survival at all. This up-step gives you a clue as to the overall god-job for you, if you choose to join, and these divine children. You will be developing the future garden for them to grow in.

"What if I don't decide to join?"

If you don't, you are just as big a part of this immense detailed, extraordinarily beautiful, all-encompassing plan. You will simply get a different god-job. Anything is possible, as you ask, give permission and choose.

"I'm confused. If it's good, regardless of what I choose, how will I know what to do?"

Follow what feels good to you. This may be joining with Anna and Michael, and it may not.

"Oh? Isn't that what you have been promoting this whole book?"

Yes, because that's my job. Other people will have other jobs. Not everyone will be called to this work, and that's for a good reason. They will carve out their own god-jobs. All people fit perfectly into the development of a good, good, good future for this planet. Far beyond survival, and even thriving, Michael and Anna have targeted Earth as a place of creation. Brand new experiments will be made on all living things. In a sense, Earth is to be a laboratory.

"Wow. That sounds amazing, but right now I am feeling incredibly sorrowful for all people who have unwittingly held suffering that was not of their own creation."

Ultimately they will know that it helped them progress on their path of individual Christhood. Every single person on the planet today is being groomed for that.

"I feel that. While I was reading this book, I was feeling lots of times that I had already said, 'Yes.' "

You said, 'Yes' to progressing on your path.

"I really felt called, like I didn't have any choice."

You were called. Every single person on this planet is called. Not everyone answers, although eventually, after they pass on and meet us, they likely will choose us. This is all perfectly timed. Part of this path is trusting in the perfection of all beings at all times. Another way of looking at it is that whatever is going on, our loving Creator parents are filling the gap, even if we don't realize it on this plane.

You said you've been dedicated to your path. Chances are you would have been given a choice to join with Anna and Michael even if you hadn't read this book. It will happen to people who have never heard the name Anna or Michael until it is spoken in their minds. Even the warranting of your eternal life can be done directly by Anna and Michael with you, just like they did it with me in the first place. You do not need any more information or help from me. It is all contained in this book.

The process is simple: ask Anna and Michael for their help, give them permission to work with you, offer your life, and make time for it to happen. Your speed of embodiment depends on the frequency and sincerity with which you do these four things.

"You mean I have to do them more than once?"

You don't have to warrant your eternal life more than once. However, your commitment may waver. You may want to back out, or look for reasons to put your efforts elsewhere for periods of time. Your lessons will cycle. In phases you will be scared, elated, impatient, selfish, brave, single-minded and then scared again. And more. Sooner or later, many of your yeses will turn into nos. Then, as you grow, your nos will eventually turn into yeses.

My suggestion is to just keep saying, 'Yes.' I so look forward to working, living and playing with a tribe of others who are joined. In the next section, we are going to give you a taste of what fun this can be.

Carry yourself forward. Your feelings are flowing naturally.
You have completed the lessons you came here for.
What's next?

It's time to unleash the power of your creative intelligence.

Chapter 16

Dare To Dream

The planet is healed. It turned out that the greenhouse gas emissions, once they were stopped, provided for a temperate climate, allowing for a full vegetarian diet.

Anna and Michael have a vision, bits of which sound like a dream to me. I empower this dream by sharing it with you because I know how important it is to open up our belief systems. For example, trainers of healing dogs can now teach puppies 90 distinct words by the time they are three months old. Why didn't I do that with my dog? Because I didn't know it was possible.

If the doggy brain can be tapped, think of what we can do with our creative imagination. Everyone knows we only use a small portion of our brain potential. When we join with Anna and Michael, they will develop that potential. Dare to dream. The human mind is able to create anything. Nothing is impossible. I wouldn't even write down the following visions if I wasn't convinced that they will somehow happen sooner than we think.

Much of Anna and Michael's vision is a common dream that some brave souls have courageously experimented with in recent decades. It's also a dream to which almost anyone I know would say, "Wow, if only that were possible."

It is. I'll paint you a picture, and you can fill in the gaps.

Groups of us who are joined to Anna and Michael are living happily in a vibrant community, sharing gardens and taking care of animals, working together and caring about each other's spiritual path as part of their own. There's not too many of us in one setting, but there are pockets of us all over the world. In each setting, we respond uniquely to our geography, and to the individual personalities we are bonded with, but we all share the same Creator Parents. We use them to help us, to guide us and to communicate between our tribal stations. Experience has taught us to revere them.

They teach us new ways of growing food, and productive, energizing and challenging ways to manufacture various items for our simple convenience. Clothing we create from wools we harvest from our pets and other living creatures. We each live in a humble abode with our blood family, or with others as dear to us as blood family. Yet the bond between each of the families is strong. We share. We help each other. We celebrate and play. We care.

Our prime values are home, children, play, learning, growing and maturing ourselves. Creativity, invention and experimentation are prioritized. Mistakes are celebrated, and forgiveness is assumed. We love each other's differences, and also share our common goals, which are to be healthy, happy, and hearty.

Nature provides all we need. We work to keep our lifestyle sustainable, and even exemplary, so that we can teach visitors our ways. We have animals who help us, joyfully, in the labour of our fields. We have playmates who are experimental versions of animals that will live, someday, on a future planet as conscious beings developing their moral choice. To spark your ideas about these animals, read Vladimir Megre's tenth book *Anasta*. Dare to expect that the quantum leap in evolutionary biology that comes with Divine children will ripple into all of Life.

Although we are harmonious, we still have to grow through various interpersonal conflicts as they arise. With Anna and Michael helping us, we up-step our creativity to find win-win solutions. With them, we have developed guidelines around romance, parenting and warranting our eternal lives to a specific mate. We have schools that teach our children how to grow food, take care of animals, develop themselves through sport and games, and befriend the spirit beings and forces around them. As the children get older, they teach the younger children. Our intellects are finely tuned to invent new solutions for making life easier and more fun, and to manifesting the various visions of Anna and Michael. When one of us is weak, infirm or in seclusion, the rest of us happily fill in the gaps.

Art, culture, entertainment and beauty are proudly displayed and admired in every home. We have time to make these creations. We gather together regularly to share meals, to make group decisions, and to re-align our roles and responsibilities. Just for fun, we like to change things up.

Learning has become a game. Memorization happens, but is not required. The most important learning comes from people working, playing and living together. How to get along harmoniously is part of it, but how to optimize the creation we are gifted with is paramount: our unique personality. How do we flower, engage, value and appreciate each individual for their contribution? The environment we are in is but a stage for that. Sensitivities are not only allowed, but encouraged.

Technology is part of this picture. Certain communities specialize in just that. Common vehicles are used to transport life essentials from one community to another. What are these essentials? They are people, those designated as messengers and teachers. Sharing with other communities is how each community will benefit from, and serve, the other.

Free energy is what we use for heat and other conveniences. Other technologies will have been invented, via Michael and Anna, to keep our lifestyle at least as good, convenience-wise, as it is today. Suffering is not required. We lose none of the advantages of the lifestyles we enjoy today. We do lose the disadvantages.

The planet is healed. It turned out that the greenhouse gas emissions, once they were stopped, provided for a temperate climate, allowing for a full vegetarian diet. We husband animals, but we no longer kill them. How could we kill someone we can reason with?

Via Anna and Michael, we have developed some telepathy, and are developing that ability in animals as well. When we have children, we start communication with them, verbally, in our minds, as soon as they are born. We have been altered to allow this; the new children that are born have it already. They are Divine Christ children, and they will be our teachers.

This dream is possible. You have leapfrogged eons of development because we decided to join early. The era of Light and Life that we would have struggled to achieve light years in the future is available now. Why? Because y/our planet has the perfect conditions for a new experiment. The creation of heaven on Earth.

This was foretold by Jesus. With this return of Christ in many bodies, it is established. We have learned much about how to develop each of you, through our experience with Anna Michael Krista. We now know that it is fully feasible. Have you ever loved as much as you wanted to?

"No," you say in a small voice.

We know. We are you. We experience every nuance of every one of your thoughts and feelings. Your bodily pain is felt by us. We would like to say thank you. It has been preordained. This planet is a disaster, no. It is a disaster of our creation, yes. That creation is the fodder that was required for this miraculous announcement to be made. Every single aspect of your planet that you abhor is carved by us to be an aspect that will drive the kingdom of heaven on Earth. Just like your own failings are carving your unique gifts, the problems of Earth are hidden treasures. With our presence, you will soon see vast, sweeping changes for the good of all. It is now fully achievable, and assured, that poverty, disease, pestilence and other horrors will, over a much shorter time period than otherwise would have been, cease to exist on Earth.

Love foolishly. It sounds crazy, but each time you say, 'Yes' to loving, once again, despite, even though, and anyways, you say, 'Yes' to this dream. Love like a new puppy. That is the concluding instruction of this book.

"Yes, but ... I want to know more."

You will, in time. I am to write more books. Those of us who are joining locally will be creating a community along these lines, with the help of Anna and Michael, in southern British Columbia. *The Way Of Alive*™ Foundation will support this work, eventually worldwide. All proceeds from this book, and from any work I do, will go to it, and donations are gratefully accepted. Learn more, and contribute your ideas to the forum, at **www.thcwayofalive.org.**

If you feel called to, I invite you to join us. There is much more fun to be had. Regardless, I encourage you to trust others, have faith in your own goodness, and hold your version of this dream sacred. Never stop working toward that, please.

www.ingramcontent.com/pod-product-compliance
Lightning Source LLC
Chambersburg PA
CBHW060246100426
42742CB00011B/1657